111 DAYS

A PARALYSIS STORY FROM FALL TO RISE

MOHAMMED WASIF HUSSAIN

This book is my attempt to give back.

It is a tribute to the friends and family who stood by me.

To the strangers who whispered prayers on my behalf.

To colleagues at work for giving their unconditional support.

To every known and unknown person during my journey.

For 111 days, I walked through darkness, but I was never truly alone.

This book is a tribute to each and every one of you.

Contents

Introduction   *vii*

The Descent

  1. Fall   3

  2. Prior To The Fall   5

  3. Day 1 Continued...   9

The Hospital

  4. Emergency Room   17

  5. Intensive Care Unit (ICU)   20

  6. Ventilator   25

The Alexithymia

  7. Suffering And Dreams   31

  8. Tracheostomy   36

  9. Long, Chaotic Dream   46

The Life Or Death Situation

  10. IVIG Second Dose   61

  11. All Hopes Lost   68

  12. Visiting Time   77

  13. Lab Rat   83

The Stabilizing

  14. Alhumdulillah   91

  15. Farewell, Dear Brother   97

  16. Airlift   105

The Homecoming

  17. Pathetic Experience   113

  18. Rehab   122

  19. Rebirth   132

Contents

20. Rise 138

Epilogue 143

Introduction

"Read a book!"

"Make reading a habit!"

"Why don't you start reading more?"

"Need a book suggestion?"

Growing up, these words echoed throughout my life, from childhood to young adulthood. It seemed everyone around believed in the magic of books, but for me, that magic always felt just out of reach. No matter how hard I tried, reading often felt like a chore, sometimes even a struggle. Little did I know that one day, I would be on the other side, attempting to write a book myself—and learning just how challenging that journey would be.

When I finally started writing, I discovered that reading and writing were worlds apart. Reading lets you sink into someone else's thoughts and feelings, following their story, their emotions, and their carefully crafted world. Writing, however, is entirely different. It is a process that requires you to dig deep, to confront your own memories, and to shape those experiences into words that others can feel and understand. Writing demands a raw honesty and vulnerability—a willingness to relive moments you may have tried to forget. It requires courage, the kind that pushes you to open up your heart and mind, knowing that every word you write is a small part of yourself that you're giving to the world.

But, why did I decide to write this book?

INTRODUCTION

Because, my life took an unimaginable turn.

There was a time when everything seemed perfect. I was healthy, happy, and fulfilled. My days were bright, my path clear. But in an instant, everything changed—a blow so devastating that it shattered the reality I thought I knew. I went from joy to sorrow, from health to illness, from strength to complete vulnerability. In those dark days, I felt as though everything I had taken for granted was stripped away.

I became gravely ill – paralyzed actually, leading to a long hospitalization, bedridden for over two months. Physically, I fought my way back to health over nine months; emotionally, the journey is still ongoing.

Yet, amidst the pain and despair, I began to learn. Oh yes, I learned—more than I ever thought.

Those days were not only difficult but also profound teachers, filled with lessons I had never sought but desperately needed.

I learned about resilience, about the power of prayer, the unwavering support of family, and a strength I never knew I had within myself. I learned that with every hardship, there truly does come ease, even if it feels like it may never come. Hardship tests us, yes—but it also brings us growth and strength in ways we couldn't have imagined.

Somewhere in between healing and learnings, a friend from the US planted a seed of an idea in my mind.

"You should pen down this episode of your life," she said, "while it's still fresh in your memory."

INTRODUCTION

And so, the thought took root. What started as a simple documentation of my experience slowly developed into a story, and before long, I felt compelled to transform it into a book and share this journey with others.

Honestly, this book does not offer mind-bending revelations or grand motivational lessons. Instead, it tells a simple, honest story—**a** story about my journey through the confinements of **paralysis** and the unimaginable hardships I faced. It captures the raw, day-by-day realities of my struggle, the moments of despair, and the quiet triumphs that marked my path to recovery.

This is a **story** from despair to resilience, **from** darkness to light, and from weakness to strength. A story of what really happens when a person **falls** **to** their lowest and, against all odds, finds the strength to **rise** again.

The Descent

CHAPTER 1

Fall

Day 1

27 April 2023 – I woke up to the familiar blare of my alarm, the morning sunlight filtering softly through the curtains. As I swung my legs over the edge of the bed, a strange heaviness settled into my limbs, as though gravity itself had somehow intensified overnight. I pushed myself to stand, but the moment I did, a wave of unsteadiness hit me. My balance wavered, and my body felt sluggish, almost disconnected from my intentions.

Confused, I sat back down, taking a deep breath as I tried to shake off the unfamiliar feeling. After a brief pause, I shrugged it off, assuming it was nothing more than lingering grogginess from a deep sleep. With a quick shake of my head, I stood up once more, determined to get on with my day.

I lived in a modest room on the sixth floor of a nine-story building— each floor was nearly identical, a small ecosystem of lives intersecting yet largely independent. My room—one of the four rooms in the shared flat, was simple, just enough space for a single bed, a small closet, and a nightstand by the window. The bathroom, shared with the others, was just outside my door, next to the kitchen.

Though my flat mates - people from different parts of the world - were respectful and kind but we rarely crossed paths beyond polite greetings and the occasional chat. My work schedule kept me busy, with long days that left little time for socializing in the apartment. This morning, as I grabbed my toothbrush and headed to the bathroom, I was determined to shake off the odd heaviness that lingered.

But as I made my way from the sink to the toilet, my legs betrayed me. Suddenly, I crumpled to the floor, the cold tiles jolting me fully awake. My heart raced, a hint of panic creeping in as I struggled to pull myself upright.

"Are you okay?" came the concerned voices of my flat mates from the kitchen.

"Yes, I'm fine!" I called back, though my voice sounded strained, even to my own ears. After a few moments, I managed to sit on the toilet seat, my hands gripping the edges for stability as I tried to calm my racing heart.

I brushed my teeth, splashed water on my face, but each movement felt foreign, unsteady. My body seemed to resist every effort. Skipping the shower I had planned, I slowly made my way back to the room, easing myself onto the bed as I dressed in my work uniform.

As I finished, a realization crept in—something was very wrong. This wasn't just a rough morning; it felt like the beginning of a much deeper struggle.

CHAPTER 2

Prior to the fall

I worked as a manager of a small clinic situated in the heart of Dubai. Leading a devoted team of eight doctors, nine nurses, and five receptionists, my role has been both challenging and deeply rewarding. My goal from the beginning was to create a workplace where everyone felt valued and connected, family-like atmosphere within the clinic, where mutual respect and teamwork became the foundation of our daily operations.

Over the past five years, I've worked across five different clinics and locations within the organization, which had allowed me to form meaningful relationships with my colleagues. Rather than viewing them as mere coworkers, I've come to see them as friends and an integral part of my life. Every team member has left a unique imprint on me, as we've shared countless experiences—from participating in cultural festivals and celebrations to enjoying team outings and gatherings. These shared moments have strengthened our bond and fostered a sense of community that goes beyond the workplace.

That month, from April 4th to 8th, I battled an intense fever that left me weak and exhausted. The high doses of medication were meant to help, but they came with their own challenges—frequent diarrhea and an overwhelming sense of fatigue. It was the month of Ramadan, and I had to forgo fasting during those five difficult days, which only added to my feelings of frustration.

By Sunday, I finally felt a glimmer of improvement and returned to work, eager to reclaim some normalcy. I threw myself back into the daily grind—clinic operations, meetings, and trainings—yet, beneath my composed exterior, I grappled with excruciating pain in my legs, a torment that refused to relent. During meetings, I found myself venting to colleagues about the unbearable ache,

"You've become *budda* (old)," my friend teased, and we laughed, momentarily burying the turmoil in that moment.

In defiance of the agony, I continued fasting through the day and spending evenings with colleagues at Iftar gatherings. Almost every night, I found myself at an Iftar party—sometimes in the clinic, other times outside with friends. These gatherings became a bright spot, a chance to shake off the lingering fatigue and the persistent pain in the legs and reconnect with the familiar rhythms of Ramadan.

Despite my high spirits, fasting took its toll. My body grew visibly thinner, and I felt weaker with each passing day. But I held onto my resolve, determined to keep my spirits high and push through on sheer willpower.

On April 19th, I received news that lifted my heart—I was granted a visa for the Kingdom of Saudi Arabia. The excitement was overwhelming; I would be able to celebrate Eid with my sister, nieces, and brother-in-law.

The next day, still riding the wave of joy, I walked through countless shopping malls, gathering gifts and treasures for my family. I filled an entire suitcase with toys and presents, carefully choosing each item with my nieces in mind. My heart swelled with anticipation, imagining the smiles on their faces as they tore open their gifts.

On April 21st, I traveled to Riyadh by air. The visit was a much-needed escape filled with laughter and warmth. During the day, we stayed at home, filling the hours with simple joys. We lounged around the living room, watching TV and laughing at familiar shows, while playing with my niece. When the TV wasn't on, we reminisced, sharing stories from our childhood and recounting memories that had somehow grown even sweeter with time. Every story sparked another, and we found ourselves lost in laughter, piecing together fragments of the past and cherishing the comfort of being together.

In theevenings, we enjoying delicious dinners at local restaurants and popular food chains, indulging in vibrant dishes that brought a smile to my face. One evening, we all went to a charming outdoor Barbeque buffet, the scent of grilled meats and spices wafting through the air as we shared stories and jokes, the atmosphere alive with joy.

We also made a trip to the beach, where the sun kissed our skin and the sound of waves created a soothing backdrop. My niece and I built sandcastles, and we all splashed in the water, laughing as the waves chased us back to shore. Those moments felt like pure bliss, a reminder of the unique warmth and joy of family—the effortless togetherness that made everything feel right.

However, the trip was short-lived. On my return to Dubai on the 24th, I twisted my ankle, a painful mishap that demanded my full attention. I limped with a painful leg all the way from Riyadh's King Khalid International Airport to Dubai International Airport, then onto the metro, a bus, and finally home. Thankfully, the next morning, the pain had subsided, but I couldn't shake the feeling that my body was trying to tell me something.

The following days, particularly the 25th and 26th, brought a new wave of weakness. My knees felt unsteady, as if they might give out beneath me at any moment. I brushed it off as lingering fatigue from my earlier illness or my recent trip, continuing to work despite the discomfort.

On the 26th, I was working as usual in my cabin and heard noises of the staff calling for help, a patient started having a seizure. I ran outside and helped him with a wheelchair. In the chaos, I felt my strength falter, and I nearly fell. Somehow, I managed to keep my balance, but it left me shaken.

Later that day, I spoke with one of our doctors about the strange sensation in my knees. He assured me it was likely due to the weakness I had been experiencing and advised me to eat properly. I left the conversation feeling a mix of relief and concern, wondering if this was just the tip of the iceberg.

CHAPTER 3

Day 1 Continued…

I lived just a short 4 to 5-minute walk from the clinic, a commute that made my daily routine feel effortless. Each morning, I set out along the pavement, passing beneath towering buildings that lined the road, their windows reflecting the first light of the day. The sounds of city life—honking cars, the distant hum of construction—became my familiar backdrop. I crossed a large traffic junction at the signal, waiting with a small crowd of pedestrians as cars zoomed past, their headlights and taillights creating streams of color in the morning bustle. Just beyond the traffic light on service lane was the clinic—my second home.

But that day, going down the elevator and walking out of the building felt like a monumental effort, and a creeping fear settled in—I worried I might fall with every shaky movement forward. I forced myself to take it slow, carefully composing myself with each step, trying to hold onto what little strength I had.

With an umbrella in one hand, I walked cautiously, sometimes reaching out to touch the cool, rough walls of the buildings on the left, grounding myself. I wore sunglasses, yet even through the dark lenses, the bright morning light seemed muted and flat, casting a dull glow over everything. It was as though the whole city had dimmed, mirroring the way my own energy was fading, step by step, with every agonizing second.

What was usually a brisk 4-minute walk stretched to over 23 long minutes. Twice, I paused at the traffic lights, not just to wait for the signal but to catch my breath, leaning against the metal pole for support and trying to steady my racing heart.

Upon arriving at the clinic, I went straight to see our most experienced general physician. After describing my symptoms, he immediately pointed out that this was likely a neurological issue, not just a consequence of weakness. He urged me to visit a neurologist as soon as possible.

Feeling a wave of concern wash over me, I stepped out of his room and sank into a nearby chair, contemplating my next move. My insurance required that I first see a general practitioner at another clinic before visiting any specialist, and the thought of navigating this process while feeling so weak was overwhelming. Just then, the doctor exited his office and told me to take someone along for support, emphasizing that I shouldn't go alone.

"Do you understand?" he asked, looking for my confirmation. "Do not go alone."

I've always prided myself on being strong and independent, so I hesitated to call anyone for help. Instead, booked a cab and while walking towards the exit door, in the clinic's hallway, my legs suddenly gave way, and I stumbled, barely managing to keep upright. A support staff noticed and rushed over, catching me just in time.

"What happened?" the nursing in-charge asked from her desk, her voice full of concern. I forced a smile, trying to downplay my worry.

"Nothing, I'll be right back," I assured her, though my words felt hollow. With the support staff by my side, I made it into a cab, grateful for the chance to sit.

Arriving at the other clinic, I struggled to get out of the cab and stand, feeling my strength draining. I called out to a passerby for help, and he kindly walked me to the clinic's entrance. Climbing the steps was an ordeal, but with his help, I finally entered the reception area.

The receptionist, who knew me well, looked up in surprise, "Is everything alright?" he asked.

"My legs are hurting," I explained. "I just need to see the general practitioner."

The waiting area was occupied by two other patients, but without hesitation, he handed me a token and rose from his seat to guide me to the Vitals room.

The nurse there checked my temperature and blood pressure. "What happened?" she asked, concern filling her eyes.

"Just some leg pain," I replied, but she knew me too well to leave it at that. Without delay, she went to speak with the doctor, returning moments later to escort me to her room, holding my hand gently for support.

"I saw other patients waiting—let them go first," I said, hesitant to take up the doctor's time. The nurse shook her head. "No, you can see the doctor now; she's free."

I sank into the chair across from the doctor, and for the first time, let it all out. I recounted everything, from the fever and diarrhea earlier that month, to the strange sensations in my legs and fall earlier that morning. She listened intently, nodding with understanding, and when I finished, she simply handed me a referral letter for a neurologist.

The specialist clinic was close by—just a short walk across a traffic signal. On any other day, I would have easily made the trip on foot. But that day, even the thought of crossing that signal felt overwhelming. So, instead, I called a cab, knowing I needed every bit of strength I had left just to reach the clinic.

Before I even exited, the GP went above and beyond, contacting the neurologist directly to explain that my condition was deteriorating and I needed immediate care. On my way to the specialist clinic, I received three calls from the neurologist's nurse urging me to come as soon as possible.

When I arrived, I was pleasantly surprised to find that the Specialist Neurologist, who typically started her shift at 1 PM, had come down early just for me. In addition the clinic team had already taken prior approval for my consultation.

I was well-liked and well-known among my peers, and as I navigated the clinic, several colleagues – Floor supervisor, support staff, Nurses and others - offered their assistance and helped me walk suggesting I get on a wheelchair. However, stubbornness kept me from accepting help—I convinced myself that this was a temporary setback, that I would be walking easily again soon.

In the consultation room, I lay on the examination bed, my body tense with apprehension. The specialist began her assessment, tapping along my legs, tapping my knees with a small hammer, and drawing lines on the skin of my feet with a sharp object. The room was eerily quiet; not a single word was spoken, only the faint sounds of her tools against my skin. The exam felt like it lasted an eternity—15 or 20 minutes stretched out in that heavy silence, each movement adding weight to the air.

When she finally finished, she stepped away, her expression unreadable. Without hesitation, she called for a wheelchair. She motioned for me to sit, but I resisted, trying to assert some independence. Her face grew serious, and she fixed me with a steady gaze.

"Who do you have here from your family?" she asked.

"I live alone," I replied.

She pressed further. "Any relatives?"

I hesitated, then answered, "Yes, my brother-in-law."

Her tone shifted, firm and direct. "You need to call him right now and go to the hospital to admit yourself and start an IVIG treatment. You have GBS. I'll inform the doctors there. Go immediately."

Her face remained set, without a trace of softness. I nodded, a heavy realization sinking in as I processed her words. As I came out of the room in a wheelchair—a reality I deeply resented, a nurse rushed over with a set of car keys, saying she'd arranged for someone to drive me to the hospital. I declined, determined to do this on my own. I took the referral letter for the hospital, quietly booked another cab, and left.

On the way, a sense of dread filled me, and I couldn't help but look up GBS on my phone. The description was alarming: a rare condition in which the immune system attacks the peripheral nerves, leading to paralysis. The weight of that realization settled heavily on my shoulders as I braced myself for what lay ahead.

Guillain-Barré Syndrome (GBS) is a rare neurological disorder where the body's immune system mistakenly attacks the peripheral nerves—the nerves outside the brain and spinal cord.

- **Symptoms**

Symptoms include muscle weakness, tingling, numbness, pain, and difficulty breathing or swallowing. Symptoms usually start in the legs or back and can spread to the arms, face, and upper body.

- **Causes**

GBS can be caused by a number of things, including viral infections, injury, or a reaction to an immunization. While the exact cause isn't fully understood, the immune response triggered by the infection appears to mistakenly attack the nerves as well.

- **Treatment**

There's no cure for GBS, but treatments can help reduce symptoms and speed up recovery. Treatments include apheresis or plasmapheresis, intravenous immunoglobulin (IVIg), and other treatments to reduce inflammation.

- **Prognosis**

Most people with GBS recover over time, but some may have weakness that persists after recovery.

The Hospital

CHAPTER 4

Emergency room

In the midst of uncertainty, I was reminded of one of life's true treasures: the friends we make. As I arrived at the hospital, apprehensive about how I would manage to walk inside, I spotted my colleague and friend waiting for me. He came running over, a look of concern etched on his face.

"Why dint you call me?" He asked,

I said, "I thought you would be busy and did not wanted to trouble anyone"

"Let's get you in a wheelchair," he suggested gently, but I refused, determined to walk alongside him. He explained that my manager, had informed him of my condition, prompting him to drop everything and come to my aid. I was touched by his support, realizing the neurologist or any of the staff from specialist clinic must have reached out to my manager.

As we entered the large hospital, the busy reception desk was the first thing we saw. I approached it and asked for directions to the emergency department. The staff guided us down a corridor, and as we neared the emergency entrance, I recognized a familiar face—a colleague who knew me well. Spotting me, he wasted no time, quickly fetching a wheelchair and insisting I sit, despite my reluctance. I could feel my strength fading, so I agreed, settling into the wheelchair as he wheeled me through the bustling hall.

I handed over all my referral documents and ID card, and within minutes, he returned with the paperwork for a reserved bed in the emergency ward. He guided me into a shared hall with four beds, each separated by curtains. My bed was near a window, though it remained closed.

Moments later, another friend and colleague arrived. She approached with a lighthearted grin and asked, "Yes sir, what have you done to yourself now?" I couldn't help but laugh, grateful for the brief moment of humor that lightened the heaviness in the room. We chatted, exchanged jokes, and even snapped a few selfies, the small bit of normalcy offering comfort in a moment of uncertainty.

Before long, the hospital's neurologist, came to examine. As he spoke, I began to feel a dullness wash over me, becoming increasingly oblivious to my surroundings. The Doctor ordered an immediate MRI and a series of tests. My friend accompanied me to the MRI room, helping me change into a hospital gown, his presence a comforting constant amid the chaos.

The MRI was a terrifying experience, filled with loud, jarring noises that seemed to reverberate through my entire being. Despite the headphones, the cacophony was overwhelming, and fear began to creep in. After what felt like an eternity, nearly 40 minutes later, I emerged from the machine feeling drained and dazed. But before I could rest, I was taken for a Nerve Conduction Test to check the nerve damage in my body, I kept making small talk with everyone I interacted with, and trying to keep my cool, but judging from the look on the technician's face the progression was rapid and alarming.

When I returned to the emergency bed, I lay down and think I managed to drift off for a short time. When I opened my eyes, I was greeted by the familiar faces of my manager and several doctors from my clinic, along with a few nurses.

"Be strong", one Doctor said with a worried face. They each offered words of encouragement, urging me to be brave, though I sensed they knew the gravity of what was to come.

From that point, my memories became a blur and the next thing I remember was being rushed to the ICU. I caught a glimpse of my clinic's Dermatologist and GP, who had come to check on me, but they missed by mere seconds, racing past in the opposite direction as I was wheeled away.

CHAPTER 5

Intensive Care Unit (ICU)

The time spent in the ICU was the scariest of my life. Even now, I can hear the relentless beeping of the monitors echoing in my mind. I felt utterly dependent, helpless, and scared—confused, worried, and in excruciating pain. Sadness and misery enveloped me, leaving me feeling weak and dejected. Honestly, I don't think I can ever fully express what that time in the ICU was like.

Day 2 and 3

I opened my eyes to a nurse's voice gently calling me to wake up—I can't recall her name. Lying there, I felt the weight of machines monitoring my pulse and blood pressure, yet I couldn't feel my legs at all. I was slipping into paralysis, and the looming question for the doctors was how far it would progress.

Though my hands still functioned, I reached for my phone, hoping to make a call or check messages. Before I could unlock it, the manager at the hospital, appeared with zam zam water. She spoke softly, urging me to contact someone from my family. I hesitated, not wanting my family in India to worry, but they insisted, and I finally agreed to call my brother-in-law.

"What exactly happened? Tell me clearly." with genuine concern my brother in law asked. I tried to brush it off and kept my response short.

"It's nothing," I said, attempting to sound casual. "Just... come to the hospital." but after that, exhaustion overtook me, and I dosed off again.

The next time I woke, my phone was ringing—it was my brother. With what little strength I had, I answered,

"Please... don't tell Mom and Dad," I murmured, my voice trembling. "They're too old and too fragile to hear that their youngest son is... getting paralyzed." The words felt heavy, slipping out with a mixture of fear and sadness as I tried to keep myself composed. Before long, exhaustion overtook me again, and I drifted back into sleep.

A male nurse gently woke me, his voice soft but insistent. "You need to eat something," he said, holding out a tray with some soft food. "I don't want to eat," I mumbled, turning my head away. But he persisted, patient and encouraging. "How will you gain energy otherwise?" he asked, moving closer and offering the food with his own hands. Reluctantly, I took a few bites, my body weak and uncooperative.

As I chewed slowly, he mentioned quietly, "You haven't passed motion in two days. I'll give you a medicine that should help." Embarrassment washed over me, intensifying the helplessness I already felt. The need for assistance in something so personal felt like an invasion, deepening my sense of vulnerability. But I gave him a slight nod of consent and closed my eyes, surrendering to the situation, hoping to preserve a sliver of dignity as he continued with quiet understanding.

In a fleeting moment of clarity, I spoke with my mom and sister, promising them that I would get well in a few days and return to India.

"Just give me four days, okay?" I pleaded, my voice trembling and unsteady. "I'll be back home, and please, for God's sake, don't worry."

Even as I spoke, I could feel the muscles in my face weakening, my lips slipping slightly to the right. The change was subtle but undeniable, and I hoped they couldn't hear the fear I was struggling to contain in each word.

I broke down, unable to hold back the flood of tears. The weight of everything I was facing felt unbearable, and my body trembled as I cried.

A few hours later, the nurse moved the curtain at the foot of my bed, revealing the figure of an elderly man sitting upright in the bed across from me. His gaze met mine, filled with curiosity and concern, and I could see him quietly questioning the nurse about my condition. I closed my eyes, wanting to shut out the world, hoping he wouldn't see the fear written across my face.

But the ordeal wasn't over. Soon after, as I reached for my phone to answer a call, it slipped from my fingers and landed on my body. I tried to lift it, but my hands wouldn't respond. A chill ran through me as the reality set in: my legs had gone first, then my back, and now, even my hands were lifeless. I lay there, helpless, a heartbreaking reminder of everything I was losing.

As my body grew weaker, I became acutely aware of the sounds around me—the nurses talking softly, the incessant beeping of the machines, and the rustling of curtains being drawn. My mind felt foggy, and although many people—senior managers, colleagues, friends, doctors, and nurses—came to visit, their faces and voices faded into a blur. I was caught in a disorienting vagueness, struggling to grasp the reality of what was happening to me.

grasp the reality of what was happening to me.

Meanwhile... in India

My family was devastated. The news of my admission to the ICU hit like a thunderbolt, leaving them in a state of shock and confusion. Questions flooded their minds: *Why the ICU all of a sudden? What is GBS? We spoke just couple of days back—how did this happen? He looked fine in the pictures from his Riyadh trip—what went wrong?*

My parents were overwhelmed, breaking down under the weight of uncertainty, unable to process what was happening. The house was a whirlwind of chaos, filled with sobbing and desperate attempts to comfort one another. It was a heartbreaking scene—tears flowed freely, not just from fear, but from the sheer helplessness of not knowing why they were crying.

"Go and bring my son back—go right now and bring him back to me!" my mom cried out, her voice breaking as she shouted at my brother.

CHAPTER 6

Ventilator

Day 4

Amidst the haze of confusion and fear, I vaguely recall a moment when a group of doctors gathered around my bed. Their faces were serious, and one leaned in closer, explaining in a calm but firm voice, "We need to place you on ventilator support. Your breathing muscles have become paralyzed."

The words were heavy, and my mind, clouded by painkillers and sedation, struggled to process them. My eyes remained closed, but I managed a nod yes with head.

The doctor's voice softened. "You'll feel some pressure at first, but the sedation will ease the discomfort," he reassured me. "We'll take every step to keep you comfortable."

Drifting in and out of consciousness, I murmured something resembling consent, surrendering to the inevitability of it all. As I faded again into the dark fog of sedation, I could faintly hear the doctors moving around me, their voices blending into an indistinct hum.

Days 5

In the murk and blur, I could only hear the relentless beeping of the machines, the rustle of curtains being drawn along their rods, and the muted conversations of other patients. An automatic sphygmomanometer was placed on my arm for monitoring blood pressure, its rhythmic inflation adding to my unease.

"Mmm... c'n y' rmov it?" I mumbled with the ventilator pipe in mouth.

"What? I can't understand," said the nurse.

"C'n y'u reeemooov et?" I repeated with a stretch in tone to make it clear.

Seeking my confirmation, she asked again, "You want me to remove the BP cuff?" Then, after a pause, she added, "Alright, let me check with the doctor."

My body had become so sensitive, so unbearably fragile, that even the gentle squeeze of the BP cuff felt like an assault. Each pump sent a wave of discomfort through me, amplifying the vulnerability that had settled deep into my bones. I felt trapped, as though every touch, every small sensation, was telling me how delicate I'd become.

With my eyes closed, I became aware of an aged lady who had been admitted with GBS. I overheard the doctors discussing the possibility of putting her on a ventilator too, and a sense of dread washed over me. In the distance, I heard loud banging at regular intervals, *"THUD!"*—A relentless pounding echoed through the room. Another patient, confined to a bed far from mine, repeatedly pressed the call button, a signal of urgency that echoed my own silent pleas.

My bed was shifted two or three times within the same ICU, each move unsettling me further. Once, I found myself positioned right in front of the nursing station, an almost surreal placement that left me feeling exposed and vulnerable. The familiar faces of nurses came and went, as I lay there, trapped in my own body and lost in the cacophony of the hospital.

The world around blurred into a swirl of sounds and sensations, a constant reminder of my suffering. I tried to grasp reality, but it slipped through my fingers like sand. In that dim, sterile environment, the line between consciousness and the dream world faded, leaving me adrift in a sea of uncertainty.

Day 6

A sudden surge jolted me awake, my mind stirring to the sounds of people rushing and speaking in hurried, panicked voices. I tried desperately to open my eyes, straining with everything I had, but they remained sealed shut. Through the red haze behind my eyelids, I sensed the brightness of the lights above me, sharp and glaring.

"Be quick but gentle, place him on the MRI machine." somewhere nearby, a voice instructed.

Another voice responded, "Alright, on the count of three."

I felt hands lifting me, positioning my body onto the cold, hard surface of the machine. My heart hammered in my chest, each beat echoing louder than the last, threatening to break free. The confinement, the unfamiliar stillness, felt like I was being lowered into a grave, sealed off from the world, unable to move or see. I lay there, frozen and powerless, a chilling feeling of burial settling over me as the machine whirred to life, the cacophony of disturbing sounds filled the air, making me shiver.

Just then, through the headphones, started playing the holy Quran. The familiar words washed over me like a soothing balm, calming my racing heart and grounding me in that moment. After the MRI, I was taken back to the ICU, where I was gently placed back into sleep, and the chaos of the world fading away once more.

"Open your eyes… I'm here, see?" came a familiar, soothing voice. It was my brother, who had traveled all the way from India to be by my side. His words broke through the fog in my mind, and I fought to lift my heavy eyelids, drawn to the comfort in his voice. Knowing he was there, his presence filled me with a sense of relief I hadn't felt in days. I tried, with everything I had, to meet his gaze, to show him that his journey hadn't been in vain. I could only manage a glance in his direction; I was completely paralyzed from head to toe, even my face felt lifeless.

The Alexithymia

CHAPTER 7

Suffering and Dreams

Nurses are the warriors in the battlefield of a hospital. They dispense comfort, compassion, and care without needing a prescription. But my experience with the nursing staff for the next few weeks was a complete shock; I encountered a different side of them. I understand the magnitude of their work—the exhaustion of caring for numerous patients with various conditions during long, tiring shifts—I understand it completely, but I never expected to feel so disconnected from their compassion.

Day 7 and 8

I was moved to an isolation room in the ICU, a spacious yet starkly empty area dominated by a single hospital bed at its center. To my right was the door, the only point of entry and exit, solid and imposing, with small glass windows. On the left down side of the bed was a small, modest washroom, its door partially ajar. A single couch sat against the wall, facing a large glass window covered by drawn curtains, letting in just a hint of light through the edges. To my right stood a row of cupboards, along with a small space designated for the nurses' trolleys, stocked with medical supplies and equipment.

The room's quiet, sterile atmosphere weighed heavily on me and from this point on, for the next several days, I lived through a horror that felt like a nightmare. Continuous delusions and dreams made me question everything I saw and heard. I drifted into a state of delirium, caught between reality and vivid dreams. I struggled to discern what was real and what a figment of my imagination.

"THUD!" —The banging sound, what could it be? My mind fixated on it, spinning scenarios so vivid they felt like dreams.

"THUD!"

Perhaps it was someone trapped in a small, bare room with only a bed, desperately banging on the door to signal for help.

"THUD!"

Yes, they were kicking the door with all their strength, creating that relentless noise. But why wasn't anyone listening?

"THUD!"

Or maybe it was a completely different scene—perhaps the sound signaled a blood sample being sent to the lab.

"THUD!"

Yes, the clatter could be from the test tube being forwarded, followed by a loud bang to alert the lab technician to collect it.

"THUD!"

No, that didn't quite fit.

"THUD!"

Could it be garbage bags being tossed from one bin to another, the heavy lids slamming shut and creating the echo?

Each theory played out in my mind like a puzzle, trying to piece together the origin of the noise, yet none brought me closer to certainty. The banging persisted, mysterious and maddening, as my imagination wove endless possibilities.

Amidst the confusion, I felt a persistent pain in my feet, a pain I couldn't articulate to anyone and the droll pooling in my mouth, choking, which no one seemed to care. In my frustration, I tried to make a sound "tut", pressing my tongue against the roof of my mouth to get the nurse's attention.

I oscillated between excruciating pain and the desperate prayer for relief—often wishing for death to free me from the suffering.

Day 9

My vision was blurred, rendering everything unclear, but I could hear two nurses discussing my blood tests. After a while, one of them administered injections and noted the readings on the monitor before leaving the room. I caught a glimpse of my brother during his visit, but soon he had to leave, and I was left alone for the rest of the day.

The nurses visited only when necessary. I struggled with saliva pooling in my mouth, desperate for it to be cleared by suction,

"tut" "tut" .... "tut" "tut" I made the sound several times.

Instead of assistance, I was met with irritation;

"I'm coming, okay? I have other work also," the nurse said scolding me, her tone brisk as she turned to leave the room. I watched as she exited, the sound of the door closing echoing in the quiet space, leaving me alone in the sterile silence.

I was connected to an automatic IV pump, its steady rhythm a constant reminder of the treatment coursing through my veins. But when the medication ran out, the machine emitted a loud, relentless beep, a sound that sliced through the quiet of the room. Left alone, I lay there, helplessly listening to the shrill beeping that seemed to stretch endlessly, each minute feeling like an hour. The noise filled the room, amplifying my discomfort and adding another layer to the physical pain, as if testing the very limits of my endurance.

In the Dream *- I lay in bed, paralyzed, struggling to move, and my body heavy and unresponsive. With every ounce of strength, I willed myself to get up, for what seemed like hours of trying and suddenly, I was standing—only to realize my body was still lying there, lifeless on the bed. A surge of panic washed over me as I stared at myself, unable to comprehend what was happening. I tried to scream but no sound came out.*

Desperation took hold, and I ran, bolting through endless hallways with no clear direction. My teeth began to loosen, falling out one by one, each drop heightening my terror. I couldn't stop; I ran, leaving the hospital, racing through dark streets, only to realize I wasn't alone. A man was chasing me, his footsteps growing louder, his shadow stretching closer with each passing second. I was breathless, consumed by fear, yet I couldn't stop.

I reached an enormous, empty hospital shrouded in darkness, its corridors stretching endlessly. I slipped inside, hiding in a dim room, my heart pounding, waiting in the silence, afraid to even breathe as the darkness closed in around me.

The fear was palpable, and as I hid, my heart raced. I felt trapped, both in my dream and in my helpless reality, where my body was paralyzed, yet my mind was frantically trying to escape. The loss of my teeth only deepened my sense of dread, amplifying my feeling of being completely out of control.

CHAPTER 8

Tracheostomy

A tracheostomy is a medical procedure where a small opening is made at the front of the neck directly into the windpipe (trachea). Through this opening, a tube is placed to help a person breathe if they are unable to do so on their own. This tube provides a clear path for air to reach the lungs, bypassing any blockages in the mouth or throat.

It's often used for people who need long-term help with breathing, such as patients with serious respiratory issues or those who are on a ventilator.

Day 10

I overheard the doctors discussing my condition with my brother, their words laden with urgency as they sought permission to place me on full-time ventilator support through a tracheostomy. Anxiety tightened its grip around my chest as I struggled to comprehend the gravity of the situation. Then came the moment of surrender: the anesthetic coursed through my veins, wrapping me in a soft embrace as I felt the world around me fade. My eyes grew heavy, slowly closing as darkness enveloped me.

Day 11

The nurse assigned was a rough and insensitive lady. Her approach felt harsh; when she used the suction, it was as if she were cleaning a drain, and when she tended to my body and face, it felt like she was mopping the floor. Each movement was jarring, amplifying my sense of vulnerability.

When the doctors made their daily rounds with my brother, I could see a little better and managed to nod in response to their questions. But once they left, I found myself struggling to convey my pain or any needs to the nurse. Instead of understanding, I received only harsh words and rude reprimands, leaving me feeling more isolated.

In the darkness of the ICU, I could feel the blood coursing through my veins, creating patterns with tiny moving spots of light reflecting off the retina cells. The spots began to dance across my vision, forming intricate, winding patterns as they stretched out from the corners of the room like the tendrils of a vine. They moved with a strange, hypnotic grace, weaving in and out of the shadows, creating delicate patterns across the ceiling and walls. Each tendril seemed alive, curling and spiraling as if guided by an unseen force, spreading like ethereal vines in bloom. I marveled at the sight, captivated by their fluid beauty. But the moment I tried to focus, to truly grasp their form, they vanished, leaving only faint memories of their delicate paths. I blinked, searching for them again, but they remained elusive, dancing just beyond the edge of my vision.

***In the Dream** -I was sitting in my office, typing as usual, but something was terribly off. My teeth began falling out, one by one, slipping into my hand like brittle, broken pieces. The sight of it left me hollowed and unsettled, a visible cloud of dread settling over me. Driven by desperation, I went straight to the dentist's office and sat in the cold, unwelcoming chair. The dentist examined me with a grim expression. "We'll need to put in a full set of dentures," she said, her words echoing ominously. Terrified yet resigned, I stood and moved toward the reception to pay. Standing there, an intense feeling of paranoia washed over* *me; it felt like everyone in the room was against me, as if they all harbored some dark intention. I wanted to turn and flee, but then a man—a man from a previous dream—gestured for me to follow him into a back room.*

Against my instincts, I followed, stepping inside only to realize too late that he was outside, peering at me through the doorway, and then shutting it. I banged on the door, my hands striking the cold surface as I called out in frantic pleas. Trapped, I ran in circles, dread clawing at my sanity. Finally, the door opened, and I bolted outside, only to find people staring at me from every direction, eyes fixed on me with unnerving intensity. Panic surged through me as I noticed men peering down from the terraces of buildings. This wasn't just one person—this was an entire network, a group somehow intent on abducting me. Fear overwhelmed my every thought as I sprinted down the street, dodging cars and obstacles, lights from the vehicles shone brightly in my face, my heart pounding, pulse racing and fear clung to me like a shadow, making it hard to breathe, with only one instinct left: to escape.

The chaos around me mirrored the turmoil within, leaving me feeling utterly trapped.

Day 12

The nurse assigned this day was utterly un-empathic. She moved through the room with a detached efficiency that felt more like a machine than a caregiver. If I cried out for attention, either by shifting my head or attempting to make any noise, "tut" "tut" …. "tut" "tut". She would merely stare blankly at me for a few moments, as if I were an inconvenience rather than a patient in distress. Her indifference was a palpable weight, leaving me feeling invisible and utterly alone. Even when my medication was overdue and the machine buzzed insistently, she didn't respond, allowing the noise to grate on my nerves.

"Can you please help me?" I would cry in my mind, knowing I couldn't speak or whisper. I tried to make the sound with my tongue, but all I received in return were harsh words, a dismissive wave of her hand, or a pointed glance that told me to be quiet. Her refusal to acknowledge my pain made my heart sink deeper into despair. I felt like I was screaming into a void, desperate for relief, yet receiving only silence. On this day, my frustration reached a boiling point. I longed to cry, yell, or scream, but my body betrayed me, rendering me powerless. This was the day I prayed the hardest for death, unable to bear the torment any longer.

Around midnight, I woke up, breaking through a fog of sleep to a familiar sound. As my blurred vision cleared, I realized it was a very close friend from Ajman. His eyes were filled with tears, and the question on his face spoke volumes: Why hadn't he been informed earlier? What had happened?

My brother must have taken his number from my phone and called him. He stood there in disbelief, grappling with the reality of my condition. Just a month ago, we had shared laughter during an Iftar party at his home for Ramadan. Now, here I was, lying in a hospital bed, unable to even respond.

He was the first to touch my hand, rubbing it gently as if trying to soothe not just me but his own shock. Words of encouragement spilled from his lips, but they felt distant, almost surreal.

"I have spoken with a lot of Doctors and everyone said you will recover quickly okay" he said while calling his wife through a video call, and she appeared on the screen, her voice warm and reassuring. "You'll be back to normal soon," she said, "my entire family is praying for your recovery."

As it was not regular visiting hours, a nurse entered and gently informed him, it was time to leave. He reluctantly stepped back but promised he would be there every day.

"I'll be back tomorrow" he assured and left with tears in eyes.

***In the Dream** —I lay in bed, surrounded by the soft, crumpled folds of clothes waiting to be ironed, their familiar weight a strange comfort. Yet I felt a presence, an invisible figure close by, silently tending to something unseen. I tried to peer into the shadows, but they only thickened around me, cloaking whatever—or whoever—was nearby.*

Then, above me, the ceiling transformed into a glowing screen, flickering with encrypted messages. A young man appeared, standing in the far corner, his fingers tapping out words to his girlfriend. Each message was more than text; it bloomed into a tiny animated scene, vivid with cartoons that danced to a strange, rhythmic melody. Each note and movement drew me in, and I lay spellbound, my eyes tracing the flow of their lively conversation, absorbing every playful exchange. But just as I grew comfortable in the intimacy of their world, the messages abruptly stopped. I sensed someone new had entered the room.

Panic fluttered through me. I tried to shift, to roll myself out of bed, but my body wouldn't budge. Hours seemed to pass as I fought against the invisible grip, feeling it tighten, an unseen force as relentless as gravity. I struggled to break free, but it was as if a faceless man was pressing me down, his arms a weight I couldn't escape. His hands held me fast while he remained hidden, his presence suffocating and inescapable, keeping me captive.

Suddenly, the air filled with vibrant melodies drifting in from outside the hospital window. The sounds of a concert resonated through the sterile room, a catchy rhythm pulsating and lyrics began to flow through my mind, intertwining with the notes like a river of creativity. Each line I imagined danced in perfect harmony with the infectious beat, igniting a spark within me.

At long last, after what felt like an eternity, I mustered the strength to tumble off the bed, landing softly on a heap of clothes. Determination surged within me, propelling me to push past the remnants of my invisible captor. But in a blink, the world around me shifted; I found myself in a wheelchair, wheels gliding smoothly across an unfamiliar floor as a man pushed me forward.

To my astonishment, we entered a grand wedding hall, alive with color and laughter. It was a celebration for a wealthy groom and a nurse from hospital, their love festooning the space with extravagant decorations, glimmering lights, and floral arrangements that seemed to bloom in rhythm with the music. I was wheeled to a vantage point, gazing down at the festivities, the air thick with joy and anticipation.

But something stirred within me, a fierce desire to be part of the celebration. With sheer willpower, I began to crawl out of the wheelchair, every inch an agonizing struggle. My arms trembled under the effort, muscles straining as I pushed against the luxurious fabric of my surroundings, gritting my teeth against the overwhelming weight of my body. Inch by inch, I fought to lift myself, heart pounding with every agonizing movement.

Finally, I succeeded, pulling myself up with a surge of triumph. My legs quaked beneath me, but I stood tall, a fragile yet resilient figure against the backdrop of the lively wedding. Just as I took a step forward, the entire room morphed, the walls shifting like a surreal lift. It moved slowly and I found myself in the midst of the celebration, surrounded by laughter and the clinking of glasses, yearning for a taste of joy—a bite to eat, a sip to drink.

But before I could indulge in the sweet nectar of the moment, everything around me began to dissolve into wisps of color and sound, swirling into the ether. In an instant, I was back in my hospital room, the familiar confines of my bed wrapping around me like a shroud.

The music faded, its joyful notes dissolving into the sterile beeping of the machines attached to me.

Day 13

This day wrapped around me like a heavy blanket, suffocating and unyielding. Despair seeped into my bones, a relentless weight that made each breath feel like a chore. The nurse, her presence cold and dismissive, added to my misery. She flitted in and out, either ignoring my needs or scolding me for what felt like my own helplessness. I had given up on everything.

But then, as the clock struck 11 a.m., a glimmer of hope pierced the fog. My brother arrived, punctual as always. He walked in like an angel, and with him came the light I had been missing. I felt my lips twitch into a fragile smile, the first hint of life in a while.

He stood by my bedside, his phone in hand, playing verses from the Holy Quran. The soothing melodies wrapped around me, filling the sterile room with warmth. He urged me to pray, to keep my faith, his voice a lifeline in my sea of despair.

"Be strong," he implored, his eyes searching mine for a flicker of understanding.

In the silence that followed, I felt the weight of my unspoken words pressing against my chest. The frustration of not being able to communicate clawed at me. But my brother, perceptive and patient, understood my rolling eyes and unvoiced thoughts. He began his gentle interrogation, starting from the top—"Head?"—to which I shook my head. "Hands?"—again, no. Then finally, "Legs?" I nodded, relief washing over me. It was a painstaking process, yet it was our lifeline.

He used his phone like a tool of connection, pointing to letters and patiently guiding me to form words. Each nod felt like a small victory. I managed to convey my discomfort about the pillow under my feet, but it was never enough. With limited time, I was left wanting to say so much more.

The day dragged on, the machines buzzing around me like persistent reminders of my predicament. I felt numb to their sounds, caught in a loop of despair.

In the Dream? *-I laid in bed looking the ceiling then suddenly swept up, carried on a stretcher by shadowy figures moving with unnerving urgency. Their faces were blurred, intentions menacing, as they whisked me through the hospital's sterile corridors at a breakneck speed. The fluorescent lights overhead streaked past like flashes of lightning, and all I could do was lie there, shivering in terror, powerless against the relentless motion.*

Just as quickly as it began, the scene fractured. I was no longer in the hospital but stranded on a highway beneath an empty, gray sky. Disoriented and alone, I searched desperately for any sign of familiarity, but my surroundings remained barren and surreal.

And then, without warning, the world spun again, and I was back in my hospital bed, lying at a painfully awkward angle. My arms and legs dangled off the side as though gravity itself was conspiring to pull me down. Panic surged within me; I strained against the pull, desperately attempting to realign my body, fearing that at any moment I would topple to the cold floor below.

Each movement was exhausting, sapping the little strength I had left. Just as I felt myself teetering on the brink, the nurse walked in, her expression unreadable. Relief washed over me; surely, she would see my plight and help me find some stability. But as I looked up at her, a strange sensation settled over me. Glancing back at myself, I saw that I was already perfectly aligned in the bed, every limb in place, undisturbed.

My panic subsided into a heavy silence as I realized that perhaps the struggle had only existed in my mind, leaving me questioning the boundary between dreams and waking reality.

Meanwhile... in India

My parents and siblings were thousands of miles away, powerless to be by my side. Their worry and despair permeated the air, even across the vast distance. My brother bore the weight of their grief, aware that they were suffering without being able to comfort me.

My mother, heartbroken, paced the floor of our family home, tears streaming down her face as she whispered fervent prayers.

My father, usually a pillar of strength, have felt lost and helpless, grappling with the terrifying prospect of losing a child. My siblings likely gathered together, laughter replaced by sorrow, sharing stories and memories, clinging to the times we had shared.

Prayers poured in from everyone—family, relatives, friends, and even those who barely knew me. Relatives of my friends and friends of my relatives joined the chorus, all seeking divine intervention on my behalf. It was a dark and sorrowful time for everyone involved, yet the power of collective hope began to weave a fragile thread of connection amidst the despair.

CHAPTER 9

Long, Chaotic Dream

Day 14

This day felt like an unrelenting storm, the most challenging yet. A fever raged within, each heartbeat echoing the intense heat coursing through my body. My head throbbed, and with it came a torrent of horrifying dreams that shattered me to my core. The boundaries of reality blurred, and I was thrust into a nightmarish landscape that left me terrified and lost. Images flashed before my eyes, each more grotesque than the last, wrapping me in a cloak of fear.

As the clock struck midnight, the room plunged into darkness, amplifying my sense of vulnerability. With high fever, I was alone, or so I thought, until my focus sharpened and I saw her—a nurse standing beside my bed. She was short, her presence surprisingly gentle in the oppressive gloom. Her sweet voice broke through the chaos, soothing my racing heart.

"Don't be scared, brother. I'm here," she said,

And in that moment, a burst of relief flooded through me. I think I cried a little, overwhelmed by her kindness.

Throughout the long hours of the night, she remained by my side, a steadfast beacon of comfort. Her voice was a soft lullaby, repeating those words like a mantra, grounding me amidst the tempest of my mind. She placed cold packs on my forehead and body, a soothing balm against the fever that gripped me. I could feel the warmth of her compassion, a stark contrast to the chill that I experienced with others.

Without a word from me, she removed the mucus from my mouth using suction, her actions demonstrating a level of care I had longed for. In those moments, she became my hope, the embodiment of the kindness I wished to see in all the nurses. I yearned to ask her name, to know the face of the angel who had taken it upon herself to ease my suffering.

In the Dream *-I found myself trapped in a confined room, an invisible weight pressing down on me, making every attempt to move feel futile. Outside, a lively music concert echoed, the sound wafting in from a garden behind the hospital — tantalizingly close yet impossibly out of reach. One moment, I was wandering through a vibrant wedding, listening to guests discussing their elegant dresses. The next, I was back in the hospital bed, staring at the ceiling, the same haunting song playing on repeat, relentlessly.*

Suddenly, I was under a podium, its platform looming above me as loud voices filled the air. An interview was taking place, the roar of applause and cheers pouring down like waves. The noise pressed into me, amplifying the sense of helplessness as I lay sprawled across a kitchen counter, paralyzed. Nearby, a wheelchair sat within sight—so close yet unreachable. I tried in my mind to roll over toward it, imagining countless ways to shift my weight, to move an inch, but each attempt left me trapped in the same spot, motionless.

A janitor passing by noticed me, his gaze a mixture of surprise and pity. He hoisted me into the wheelchair and pushed me back to the hospital bed. But in a dizzying whirl, I was suddenly inside a helicopter, soaring high above the city. The landscape below was alive with pinpoints of light, tiny constellations scattered across the streets. The wind whipped at me, and I felt a thrilling rush, my head hanging out of the open door as we sped from one corner of the city to another. The sensation was exhilarating, the view breathtaking.

Then, a nurse pulled me back inside, her face shadowed as she laid me beside a lifeless body, and the thrill instantly morphed into horror. Cold dread seeped into me as I felt the proximity of the corpse, an unbearable closeness that filled me with suffocating fear. My breaths came shallow and quick, each one struggling against the weight of my panic.

Two nurses moved around me, their movements mechanical and unfeeling. Without a word, they began to remove my hospital gown, slipping me into a fresh shirt and pants. But the nightmare deepened as they rolled my body directly over the corpse beside me. A wave of revulsion and helplessness flooded through me, my skin prickling with discomfort. Every nerve screamed in protest, but I was powerless to stop them.

The helicopter touched down on a sacred mountain, its grandeur overshadowed by the strange crowd that disembarked. The married couple from before had brought everyone here, and music played on a continuous loop, its rhythm filling the thin mountain air as cameras whirred and flashed from every direction, capturing every moment. I stood up, feeling the icy spray of an enormous waterfall nearby, its cascade rumbling like distant thunder as the cold droplets splashed against my face. The wind howled, whipping my hair as I squinted against the chaos of light, sound, and movement, each sensation merging into a storm of overwhelming noise.

Desperate for peace, I retreated into a small room carved into the mountainside. I lay down, longing for a moment of quiet, but a paralyzing sensation crept over me once more, rooting me to the bed. Shadows began to form, emerging from the dim corners of the room—menacing figures whose presence filled me with dread. I felt them pressing in, smoke curling around my face, their hands reaching out, pinching and poking, each touch a painful jolt. My voice cracked as I tried to cry out, each plea for mercy escaping as a muted whisper. Tears streamed down my face as I felt their relentless hands on me, grasping, holding me captive in this nightmare.

A nurse entered, and I begged him for help, my voice weak, words tangled and barely audible. He gave me a puzzled look, unable to understand, and turned away, leaving me alone with the shadows. The figures grew bolder, their grip tightening as my strength waned. The bed beneath me began to shudder, fabric tearing as the frame splintered. With a sickening crack, it gave way, and I tumbled to the cold floor, a sharp pain shooting up my side.

I heard footsteps outside and looked up to see a nurse glancing through the small window in the door. I cried out, my voice hoarse, desperation clawing at my throat, but the door was locked tight, trapping me in the room. I reached out, my voice breaking as I begged for help, but she could only watch, unable to enter.

In an instant, the entire room jolted and began to rise, carried aloft by the hum of a helicopter's blades. I felt the world tilt as we flew over a vast stretch of sea, waves churning below and a narrow bridge cutting across the water's expanse like a thin thread. My heart pounded as I clung to the edges of the room, trying to steady myself against the sensation of hovering between sea and sky.

The room descended abruptly, settling into the center of an enormous court hall. I was alone beneath a blinding spotlight, its harsh beam isolating me in a halo of intense scrutiny. Around me, judges were seated in a perfect circle, their faces shrouded *in shadow, only their eyes visible, cold and watchful. Their expressions were unreadable, but their presence felt suffocating, as though they were peering into my very soul.*

An absurd frustration took hold as I noticed my pants kept slipping, and each time I tugged them up, they would slide down again, slipping just out of my control. My annoyance grew as I tried in vain to maintain some dignity under the piercing gaze of the judges, but the fabric seemed to defy me, falling again and again, each time more aggravating than the last.

Just as I managed to pull them up once more, I felt a sudden, invisible grip lift me from the floor. I was carried upward and then placed within a narrow glass enclosure, a small, transparent room that resembled a lift. It moved quickly and suddenly taking to the scenes of possible punishments — prosecution, burning, shooting, or being fed to wild animals. Each scenario played out in a horrific loop, my mind spiraling into despair, the same song haunting my thoughts.

In the glass room now, next to me lay a dead body, shrouded in a white cloth, the weight of death hanging heavily in the air. A small boy lay beside me, his eyes locked onto mine, unblinking and vacant. Three women in black veils surrounded me, their gaze piercing and judgmental, demanding that I justify my actions. I cried out, but the words refused to form; I could only make desperate sounds, my tongue touching the roof of my mouth in a futile attempt to communicate. I felt completely broken and terrified.

The glass lift began to descend towards a small hole where animal waste awaited. I struggled to position myself properly, the stench overwhelming, and my body refused to cooperate. In my misery, I cried, feeling utterly helpless.

Then, my family was summoned for the hearing—my father, mother, sisters, brothers—all crying as they witnessed my torment. Their tears mirrored my own, a shared sorrow that felt suffocating.

I was strapped into a roller coaster, a terrifying ride through graveyards, animal farms, and cemeteries, my heart racing as I glimpsed bodies burning and heads being chopped off. The terror escalated, my pulse pounding as I faced the prospect of my public verdict displayed on massive screens for thousands to witness, thousands of eyes scrutinizing my fate, voting on whether I should live or die. And I was sobbing convincing them that I was innocent. I cried and sobbed, pleading my innocence, but unable to speak, I could only plead in my mind, hoping they could read my thoughts.

They demanded the truth from me, pressing harder with each new torment. Blindfolded, I heard the guttural grunts of wild pigs let loose, each snarl and squeal heard closing by, wreaking havoc on mind. They thrust me forward, pushing me close to the whir of enormous spinning saws, the sharp, metallic roar filling my ears as the air grew cold. With each brush against death, I felt the sting of betrayal, yet I held fast, grounded in my faith.

Then, as if to break my spirit once and for all, I was dragged before a gathering, an ominous crowd assembled with stones in hand. One by one, they cast them, each stone a silent accusation, each impact a fresh wave of agony. But amidst the jeering faces and relentless pain, I clung to my faith with fierce determination, my voice rising above the noise as I recited verses from the Quran, praying for the mercy of divine intervention.

The final act of their cruelty came as they removed my ventilator, setting a timer as though counting down to my last breath. They stood watching, certain that without support, I would succumb. Yet with every second that passed, I kept breathing, defying the odds. Time stretched, and I drew breath after breath, my life a testament to the power of faith. The onlookers' expressions shifted from confidence to disbelief, and then to awe, marveling at what seemed an impossible feat.

Against all expectation, I emerged victorious. The room fell silent, faces reflecting a mix of wonder and shock. It was as if divine mercy itself had reached out, holding me up as I proved, even to myself, the unyielding strength that lay within. That moment left them speechless, a miracle unfolding before their eyes.

Through the window, a breathtaking vision of the Holy Mecca appeared, the sacred structure glowing with an ethereal light. My heart swelled with gratitude, an overwhelming need to bow down and give thanks. Clad in only a small cloth, which slipped again and again, I mustered every ounce of strength within me to stand. Despite the frailty of my limbs, I bent my back, steadying myself long enough to bow deeply. The act, simple yet profound, echoed in my soul. In the silence that followed, voices seemed to resonate around me, saying, "He deserves an award."

Without warning, I was transported to a grand mansion—a world away from my humble room. The space stretched endlessly, with countless halls and rooms. Ornate tapestries draped the walls, and chandeliers cast soft light over spiral staircases that twisted into the distance. A vast garden unfolded outside, lush and vibrant, with a bright rainbow arcing across a clear sky, its colors dancing over fountains that sent sparkling sprays into the air. And all around, unseen figures watched me with questioning eyes, murmuring, "How did he do it?"

For another round of test, I was led down into a dimly lit basement, a cold room shrouded in shadows. The door closed, and the lights flickered out, plunging me into darkness. Fear clutched my chest as I gasped, my body shaking as I struggled to rise. Each time I tried, my legs buckled, and I fell back, but I refused to surrender. Summoning every shred of courage, I forced myself to my feet again, each attempt more determined than the last. With trembling hands, I reached for the staircase that wound up and up.

I clung to the banister, the staircase spinning in endless circles, yet somehow, I reached the rooftop. As I emerged, the vastness of the ocean spread before me, its deep blue stretching to the horizon. The wind met me, gentle yet insistent, brushing against my face and filling me with a sense of renewal. Before I could rejoice, I was back again in the basement repeating the cycle again.

Events twisted in my mind; I was in a marketplace when a fire broke out, then at a beach where I began to drown. Next, I floated in a room just as it exploded. These scenes replayed with each time a desperate attempt to escape the fire, the drowning, and the blast—yet I remained powerless to save myself.

Again, I found myself back in the basement, struggling to breathe. But I pushed through, managing to stand and climb the stairs, despite the jeers and mockery of the figures surrounding me. With sheer determination, I ascended and entered a large hall filled with many rooms. I sought solace in one of them, yearning to rest before my upcoming felicitation ceremony, utterly exhausted.

But when the time came, I could not rise. My body felt heavy, my limbs unresponsive, and as I opened my eyes, the sterile lights of the ICU came into focus once more.

The dream faded, but its haunting echoes lingered in my mind, a testament to my struggle against despair and a reminder of the strength I still had to find.

Day 15

The fever raged on, refusing to relent, and the concerned doctors ordered a barrage of blood tests, X-rays, and scans. Nurses surrounded, pricking and puncturing every available vein in my hands. I felt no pain, but the touch of the needle was unsettling, as if it were piercing not just my skin, but my very soul. New medications were introduced, including one injected directly into my belly button.

The rude nurse returned, her harsh demeanor casting a shadow over the dim room. She seemed to escape my presence at every opportunity, leaving me feeling unwanted and useless. I think I spent the day sleeping with my eyes open, unable to discern where reality ended and my gruesome dreams began. When the doctors and my brother visited at their usual times, I could barely respond, lost in an obscurity of fatigue.

Alone, I stared at the false ceiling, its large squares separated by beams that formed a disorienting pattern. I imagined an invisible string connecting one corner to another, tracing paths that only existed in my mind. In the center, a greenish square resembled a patch of carpet sprinkled with tiny LED lights. I tried to focus, hoping to discern its details, but all I could see was an indistinct outline.

As the afternoon wore on, a sense of suffocation enveloped me, accompanied by an uneasy, excruciating pain in legs. I glanced toward the door, hoping for help, but found none. Pressing my head against the bed, I felt a primal urge to scream, to let out the anguish trapped inside.

After a while, I noticed someone sitting near the door, engrossed in videos on the phone. She had been asked just to keep an eye while the assigned nurse was away. Desperate for attention, I began moving my head and making sounds with my tongue, "tut" "tut" …. "tut" "tut", hoping to catch her eye. Time stretched endlessly, and despite my efforts, she remained oblivious. Frustrated, I shook the bed, seeking even a sliver of acknowledgment.

"tut" "tut" ….

"tut" "tut" ….

"What is your problem? Just sleep quietly, stupid." In a dismissive tone, she snapped.

Her words stung, and I felt tormented by her indifference. All I wanted was for her to adjust my blanket or pillow, to ease my discomfort, but instead, I received only a standard response: "What happened? Just sleep." She didn't even approach me, remaining distant and uncaring.

After a long struggle, I finally gave up, surrendering to my exhaustion. As evening fell, I realized the rude nurse had returned, and with her came the familiar dread.

When brother arrived at 5 PM for visiting hours, I was too drained to ask for help. I felt a heavy weight in my chest, an overwhelming sense of defeat. I ignored everything around me and slipped back into the blurred lines of the real and unreal, retreating once more into the world of dreams.

In the Dream - *The events repeated like a broadcast stuck on a loop, each scene a distorted déjà vu, blurring the line between dream and reality. I moved through each scene, somehow aware of what would happen next, yet powerless to change anything.*

First, I found myself in a crowded animal market. The air was thick with the pungent smell of animals and hay, a sharpness that clung to my senses. I moved cautiously, slipping between stalls, trying to escape the eyes of a man who trailed behind me. His questions filled the air, each one sending a spike of nervousness through me. Suddenly, flames erupted from somewhere deep within the market, a raging fire that devoured everything in its path. I felt the heat licking at my skin, yet I knew it was coming. And still, I was helpless, trapped as the world burned around me.

Then, in an instant, I was on a pristine beach, the water clear enough to see shells and pearls shimmering at the bottom. Drawn by their beauty, I waded in, each step pulling me deeper into the cool embrace of the ocean. I knew I would drown, yet I couldn't stop myself, as if some unseen force propelled me forward. The water closed over my head, and I sank, powerless against the weight of the waves as they pulled me down.

Next, I was suspended in a room without gravity, floating aimlessly. The air was thick with gas, the smell cloying and suffocating. I knew there was a tiny spark waiting to ignite it all, a spark I could see forming across the room. I could have reached out to stop it, could have saved myself—but my limbs remained heavy, unresponsive. The spark came, and in an instant, the room exploded, the force tearing through the air and leaving me adrift in an endless, suffocating void.

Then came a new scene, a fourth ordeal. I was in a car, sealed tight, the air thick and stifling as oxygen dwindled. I gasped, struggling for each breath, pleading with everything I had left. Finally, a window opened, and I stumbled out, sprinting toward a nearby building, desperate for safety. But the hallways twisted and turned, leading me in endless circles. Each corner brought me back to the same starting point, as if I was running against some unseen barrier. Exhausted and frantic, I was led to a small room where the air grew thin again, a dim candle casting long, flickering shadows on the walls.

I sank into a worn sofa, feeling the weight of surrender settle over me. With every dwindling breath, the strength to resist faded. I gazed at the candle's faint glow, watching its light waver, small and fragile, like my last glimmer of will. And in that moment, I let go, slipping into the darkness, surrendering to the relentless rhythm of events that seemed to repeat endlessly, beyond my control.

The Life or Death situation

CHAPTER 10

IVIG second dose

IVIG, or Intravenous Immunoglobulin, is a treatment that involves giving a patient a concentrated dose of antibodies through an IV (intravenous) line. Antibodies are proteins in the blood that help the body fight infections. IVIG is often used for conditions where the immune system is mistakenly attacking the body's own tissues, as it can "reset" or calm down the immune response.

In this treatment, purified antibodies collected from healthy donors are infused into the patient's bloodstream. This can help protect the body and, in some cases, reduce inflammation or stop harmful immune attacks, giving the body a chance to heal.

Day 16

After a series of neuro assessments, the doctors made a critical decision: they would start a second dose of IVIG. This was not a usual protocol; it signaled just how serious my condition had become.

As the haze in my mind began to lift, I noticed my surroundings more clearly. To the right of the entrance door, a clock hung on the wall, but I couldn't quite make out the time. Looking to my side, I realized that the unseen force suffocating me, gripping tightly, was actually a steel stand supporting the ventilator tube connected to my throat. My earlier fear that all my teeth had fallen out transformed into relief when I felt them with my tongue, solid and present.

That day, the nurse had left the curtain on the glass window open. The usual sterile stillness of the room seemed to fall away as I lay there, gazing outside. Slowly, the sun began to rise over the horizon, its soft, golden light spilling into the room. The beams crept quietly across the floor, casting long shadows on the white tile and illuminating the edges of the medical equipment in a warm glow that softened their harsh lines. Monitors beeped faintly in the background, but for a moment, even they seemed to fade away.

The light reached my bed, warming my face, and in that deep, silent pause, I felt a strange peace settle over me. The room, usually bustling with hurried footsteps and urgent whispers, was still and bathed in an amber glow that felt almost sacred, as though the sun itself had reached in to touch this small, forgotten corner of the hospital. It was just a sunrise, a single moment in an endless stretch of hours. But right then, it felt like the world had slowed down just for me, offering a reminder of beauty, even here, amidst the unyielding grip of wires and machines.

The day continued with doctors making their rounds. They asked me to try lifting my hands and legs, to open my mouth and close my eyes tightly. I struggled to comply, my body feeling unresponsive. All I could manage was a slight nod, a silent acknowledgment of my limitations.

Twice a day, my brother visited for an hour, bringing updates about my family. He would sit beside me, asking if I needed anything, playing the Holy Quran softly in the background. His voice was a balm, reminding me of the love and support waiting for me outside these walls.

"Don't question Allah for what has happened," he advised gently. "Everything happens by His command."

His words instilled a sense of courage in me, a flicker of hope amid the despair. Yet, despite his encouragement, my helplessness weighed heavily on my heart. The pain, the isolation—it broke me down to a point where I found myself praying for death, an escape from the suffering that felt endless.

__In the Dream__ - I am trapped beneath layers of sheets that pulsated like a living organism. The bed beneath inflated and deflated, each rhythmic surge tightening around my body, binding me further into its depths. Panic clawed at my chest, my heart pounding like a drum, echoing the oppressive struggle for breath.

I fought against the sheets, my limbs thrashing in desperation, but they constricted like a vice, pulling me deeper into this surreal prison. Hours melted away as I writhed, feeling the weight of the world pressing down on me. I screamed for help, but my voice vanished into the void, swallowed by the suffocating silence.

Then, a figure appeared at the edge of my vision—a shadow slipping through the dim light. My heart raced with a flicker of hope. "Please," I thought, "just close the machine! End this torment!" But the figure remained indifferent, hovering just out of reach. The suspense grew heavier, thickening the air around me as my pleas faded into whispers.

Just when I thought I could endure no more, I summoned every ounce of strength and managed to twist free, grappling for the machine that kept me ensnared. My fingers found the switch, and I turned it off, a rush of triumph surging through me. But as the bed settled, I froze in horror.

There, beneath the covers, was another body—still, lifeless, in a white dress holding me in its arms, its grip tightening like a noose. He squeezed, a sinister smile creeping across his face, as if feasting on my despair.

Day 17

By now, a pattern had emerged in my days, a mundane routine that brought a strange sense of familiarity.

3:00 AM — The stillness of the ICU was interrupted as the nurse begins her early-morning routine. Soft footsteps and the faint rustling of fabric signal her presence before she arrives at the bedside. The cleaning begins—a brisk yet practiced ritual, precise in each movement. Medications are administered, one by one, their purpose barely registered amidst the haze of early-morning grogginess. The nurse's gloved hands glide methodically over equipment, documenting monitors and preparing for the day ahead.

- ALONE -

5:00 AM — The Azaan call filters softly through the speakers in the room, the sacred words filling the space with a solemn peace. The beauty of the call, as it echoes in the quiet ward, provides a few minutes of spiritual solace amidst the physical trials.

- ALONE -

7:00 AM — The first doctor arrives, a figure of authority whose presence brings a shift in the atmosphere. His footsteps are quick, his questions direct, the observations brief. He reviews charts, speaks a few words, and leaves, a whirl of efficiency.

8:00 AM — Another doctor steps in, bringing a different energy but the same sharp, clinical focus. His examination is just as swift, a blend of reassurances and instructions that seem routine to him but somehow anchoring for the patient, marking another part of the day.

- ALONE -

11:00 AM — At last, a familiar face arrives: the comforting presence of a brother. His visit like an infusion of warmth, breaking the sense of isolation. There is little conversation, just a shared presence, and the comfort of silent understanding. Even in this quiet companionship, his arrival feels like a balm, a reminder of family and home.

- ALONE -

1:00 PM — The afternoon Azaan echoes in the room, another reminder of the world outside, as the nurse arrives to feed lunch thru the tube and the next round of medications. This process is methodical, yet something in the nurse's presence can feel impersonal, almost transactional, as she tends to the mechanics of the feeding and medication.

- ALONE -

5:00 PM — Another Azaan reverberates, followed by the brother's return. This visit feels somehow softer, tinged with the gentle glow of the approaching evening. He may bring quiet stories or simple updates, his presence like a thread back to a reality beyond the sterile walls of the ICU.

- ALONE -

7:00 PM and 8:00 PM — The room fills once more with the melodic tones of the fourth and fifth Azaan. The rhythmic cadence of these calls, spread throughout the day, brings a certain structure, a pulse that underscores each hour.

- ALONE -

9:00 PM — The final routine of the day unfolds with the nurse's return, administering night medications and the last feed through the tube. The sounds grow quieter, the pace slows. The hum of monitors becomes the only company, and the ward settles into silence, leaving me alone with thoughts, memories, and a steady stream of hours until the next cycle begins.

- ALONE & ABANDONED -

12:00 AM — Around midnight, as the room fell into the deepest quiet, a figure would glide in to mop the floor, her presence barely more than a shadow in the dim light. I never saw her face, only heard the gentle swish of the mop across the tiles and the soft, rhythmic footsteps that punctuated the silence. Judging from her voice—a low hum, perhaps a song she sang softly to herself—I imagined she was a Black woman, diligent and tireless in her work, her movements steady and unhurried.

- ALONE & VERY LONELY -

In the hours between these routines, the minutes stretch into solitude. Time becomes fluid, slipping through gaps in awareness as the weight of silence fills the space. Left alone, with only the rhythmic beeps of machines and the soft glow of dimmed lights, there is a sense of hovering between wakefulness and rest.

And so the cycle would repeat, night after night, morning after morning. In the stillness, I had plenty of time to reflect on my situation, to ponder the small victories and the overwhelming challenges. Each day blurred into the next, a rhythm that both comforted and confined me.

CHAPTER 11

All hopes lost

Day 18

The fever returned, an unwelcome companion that brought with it a new wave of delusional dreams. This unsettling experience was all too familiar; fever and nightmares had plagued me before, each episode distorting reality and dragging me into a terrifying abyss.

The nurses, continued to treat me with indifference or outright rudeness. Their scolding felt like added weight on my already burdened spirit. Instead of comfort, I often received sharp words, as if my suffering was an annoyance to them. I longed for compassion but found only coldness, each reprimand deepening my sense of isolation.

In the midst of this chaos, my brothers were called to a meeting with the doctors and hospital management. They discussed the bleak possibility of transferring me to India, as they feared my condition would meet a grim outlook. But my brother was adamant, resolute in his belief that I should remain in Dubai for as long as my insurance allowed—three crucial months. He was determined to fight for my recovery, even when hope felt fragile.

Physiotherapy was introduced, a flicker of possibility amidst the despair. The physiotherapist, a short lady with a steady demeanor, approached my immobilized body with purpose. She began to move my arms and legs, stretching and folding them in an attempt to coax even the slightest movement from my lifeless limbs. Each session sent sharp jolts of pain coursing through my legs, causing me to jerk involuntarily. But I lay there, grappling with the crushing weight of my helplessness and dependence on others.

In the Dream *-I lay in a bed that resembled a vast crib, its sides towering like the bars of a prison. The mattress felt like a fur ball, enveloping me, sinking me deeper into its plush embrace. I was in my sister's house in Riyadh, the familiar scents of home swirling around me. Just as I began to orient myself, the scene shifted, and suddenly I was in a sterile hospital room, the same bed trapping me.*

Before I could process the shift, the bed lurched and began to rise. It lifted me high above the city, soaring towards the terrace of a high-rise building. My heart raced, a mix of exhilaration and dread flooding through me. The landscape beneath morphed into a tapestry of vibrant lights and bustling life, the streets alive with people dining beneath canopies of twinkling bulbs.

I soared over bridges that glimmered like silver threads, weaving between towering structures. Cars whizzed by below, their headlights creating a dazzling blur. The sensation was akin to a roller coaster—thrilling yet terrifying, each twist and turn sending a jolt of adrenaline through my veins. I flew close to the ground, skimming over roads packed with crowds, feeling the rush of wind against my skin, narrowly avoiding collision with the throngs below.

Just as quickly as it began, everything shifted again. A sudden jolt felt like someone pressing a reset button, and I found myself back in the hall of my sister's house, the air thick with nostalgia. But the cycle resumed, the bed lifting me once more, carrying me through the same breathtaking scenes—high above the city, over the bridges, and among the people, their laughter and chatter echoing like a distant symphony.

Each loop felt like a strange blend of joy and terror, a captivating dance between freedom and entrapment. I was caught in a mesmerizing spiral, the familiar comfort of home entwined with the exhilarating rush of flight.

Would I ever escape this loop, or was I destined to soar endlessly through the same vivid dreams, forever suspended between two worlds?

Meanwhile... in India

The news of my deteriorating condition spread like wildfire, reaching far beyond the circle of immediate family and friends. It seemed as if the entire community had been shaken by the gravity of my situation. My house transformed into a place of mourning, the air heavy with grief and uncertainty. Relatives from near and far poured in, offering whatever moral strength and support they could muster to my parents, who were visibly crumbling under the weight of it all.

Inside the house, the scene was heart-wrenching. Groups of people sat in hushed circles, some chanting prayers with fervent desperation, while others whispered stories of my childhood, as if those memories could somehow breathe life into the situation. My photos and videos circulated from hand to hand, igniting smiles that quickly faded into tears. My voice in the videos, once a source of joy, now felt like a cruel echo of what might be lost.

My friends, unwavering in their loyalty, visited daily, sitting quietly beside my father. They spoke softly, urging him to stay strong, to keep his faith alive despite the overwhelming darkness. Yet, my father couldn't find words to respond. He simply sat there, his face a canvas of anguish, silently wiping away his tears as they fell in an unrelenting stream.

"Nobody is listening to me! They must bring him back home. You all do something and bring him home," my dad said, his voice trembling as he struggled to hold back tears. His words were firm and the raw emotion beneath them was unmistakable.

"But Uncle, the treatment is better there. Let him get stable first," one of my friends gently replied, trying to reason with him.

Everyone, including me, believed that staying in Dubai was the best option for my treatment and recovery. The advanced medical care and resources gave me a better chance. But my dad thought otherwise. His heart couldn't bear the distance, the helplessness of not being by my side. For him, no medical facility, no matter how advanced, could outweigh the comfort of having his son home, surrounded by the love and care of family. To him, being together was the only path to true healing.

And my mother—she trembled with every ring of the phone or the doorbell, her heart leaping into her throat. The sound was enough to freeze her in place, her hands shaking as she hesitated to answer. Each time, she feared it would bring the worst news, news that would shatter whatever fragile hope she was clinging to. Her face bore the weight of sleepless nights and silent prayers, a mother fighting an invisible battle against despair.

Every corner of the house seemed to bear the weight of sorrow, every sound—a prayer, a sob, a whispered recollection—was soaked in an unbearable mixture of fear and helplessness. It wasn't just my family that grieved; it was as if the entire world around us had paused, holding its breath for news, for a miracle.

Day 19

The day flew by in the same pattern, a blur of moments that felt endless merging into nearly three weeks of torment that had broken me down. I lay there, gazing at the intricate web of tubes and machines that clung to my body, each one an unwelcome tether anchoring me to this bed.

From the top, a feeding tube was shoved into my nose, reaching my stomach.

The throat was punctured by a tracheostomy, the ventilator's tube connecting the machine filling breaths in me.

Electrodes were attached to my chest connected to the ECG machine, monitoring my heart beat like a fragile thread.

Both my hands bore IV cannulas, the veins marred by countless needle pricks, each one a reminder of my vulnerability.

A pulse oximeter clamped onto my left finger for monitoring the heart rate.

And a urinary catheter linked to a collection bag.

Though my body felt no physical pain, the mental weight of these tubes and wires pressed upon me like an invisible shackle, chaining me to a bleak and unending existence.

Day 20

As the nurse came to clean me and change the sheets, I could see more clearly. The green square on the ceiling revealed itself as the blueprint of the room's design, complete with measurements. As I shifted my head from side to side, I look in the structure of the room, so different from the distorted images my mind had conjured.

The nurse moved through her routine with a mechanical precision as a robot. I watched her methodically, noting each step of the process.

Step 1: She begins by lifting the cover sheet off of me and gently removes the pillows from under my legs, setting them aside.

Step 2: Unties the threads of my gown, carefully sliding it off without disturbing the IV cannulas connected to my hands.

Step 3: Peels away the electrodes from my chest, which monitor my heart rate, and cleans the skin on my chest, hands, and legs with a generous number of wet wipes.

Step 4: Another nurse arrives to assist. Standing on my left, they each take one of my arms. The nurse on the left gently pulls my right hand to turn my body slightly, while the nurse on the right cleans my back and legs.

Step 5: They slide a clean sheet under me, folding the old one toward the center, then reposition me on the half fresh sheet.

Step 6: Switching to the other side, they repeat the process. The nurse on the right gently pulls my left hand, allowing the nurse on the left to clean my back, hips, butt and legs on this side, then slide the fresh sheet underneath, fully replacing the old one.

Step 7: Once I'm comfortably positioned on the new sheet, they reapply the electrodes to my chest, making sure each one is securely placed.

Step 8: Then she drapes my gown back over, ensuring all the tubes and wires remain undisturbed.

Step 9: She uses a cotton swab dipped in mouthwash, held with tweezers, to clean my mouth. Then, uses a suction tube to clear any mucus and drool.

Step 10: Replaces the plaster of the feeding tube on my nose, making sure it's secure.

Step 11: The pillows are replaced under my legs, and the nurse carefully covers me with a fresh sheet, tucking it in.

Step 12: Finally, she administers my medications, gives me nutrition through the feeding tube, and documents all my vital readings from the monitors.

This routine, from start to finish, takes over an hour, each step deliberate and precise.

I must take a moment to acknowledge this, despite the occasional rude or harsh behavior from some of the nurses, I would be deeply ungrateful if I didn't express my heartfelt gratitude to every single one of them, for the care and service they provided.

They were there for me during my most vulnerable moments, feeding me, cleaning me and enduring my presence.

I owe them my sincerest "Thanks" for their patience, resilience, and dedication and I will forever carry a deep appreciation for them.

CHAPTER 12

Visiting Time

Day 21 and 22

Every day, my heart clung to the clock like a lifeline, yearning for 11 AM and 5 PM—the moments when my brother would walk through that door. My eyes, heavy with pain, darted between the clock and the entrance, time blurring into an agonizing haze. When he finally arrives, a smile flickered across his face, but the worry etched in his brow and the tears threatening to spill revealed the truth.

He would arrive at the hospital at 10 AM, as if tethered to me by an invisible thread, staying until 6 PM. In the sterile, suffocating air of the hospital, he filled the silence with talks that masked his own heartache. I knew he spent those hours wandering the waiting lobby and prayer room, seeking solace, connecting with other families lost in similar despair.

"Do you need anything?" he would ask, his voice a mix of hope and desperation. I would gesture weakly toward my legs, the pain throbbing like a cruel heartbeat, and whisper for him to tell the nurse to clear the mucus from my throat, the choking sensation a constant reminder of my vulnerability.

Then he would lift his phone, connecting me to our family—parents and siblings—all of them pouring love and encouragement into the space between us. Their faces flickered on the screen, full of hope, urging me to be strong.

"Did you know a person's lifespan is decided while they are in their mother's womb?" he said looking away. I understood exactly what he was trying to imply and convey. Deep down, though fear gripped me and I was utterly terrified, I knew I was ready.

"Indeed, we belong to Allah, and indeed, to Him we return," he added, playing Quranic verses that wrapped around me like a fragile promise.

But it wasn't just my brother who visited every day. Friends came, each one bringing a different energy, each visit a lifeline in this otherwise silent world.

One friend would come and just stand by in shock, silent and solemn, his face bearing a mix of sadness and disbelief as he took in the tubes and machines.

Another friend would visit with a different approach, his words full of both sorrow and urgency. "I can't see you like this," he'd say, his voice low. "I want my happy, joyful friend back," his eyes searching, pressing the nurse with questions about my recovery, as if he could accelerate the process by sheer will alone.

My friend from Ajman would travel 45.6 kilometers—a journey of over an hour—after finishing his work, arriving late at night just to be by my side. He'd stand close, his voice soft but steady: "Tell me what's on your mind. Do you need anything? Don't worry about money—I can help, okay" His words settled over me like a calming embrace, offering a comfort I didn't know I needed.

My brother-in-law came with his friends and roommates, each of them lending their strength, but one stood out. He'd clench his fist tightly in a gesture of strength, looking directly into my eyes, saying, "Have a strong will to recover. Our will is the key—don't ever lose hope." His words were grounding, filling the room with an energy that felt like a balm, soothing the ache that had settled in.

Another friend who worked at the same hospital, brought his colleagues along, all of them hoping to lift my spirits with small jokes and laughter. "You're driving everyone crazy, you know that, right?" he'd say, attempting a smile. "Get better soon, or I swear, I'll beat you for all this trouble!" There was comfort in his humor, in the lightness he tried to bring to the room.

Doctors from my own clinic also stopped by, speaking with reassurance. "You're a strong man," they said, a quiet confidence in their voices. "We know you'll get through this."

And then there were the nurses from my own clinic, my sisters with whom I worked, despite their role, sometimes couldn't bear to stay long. They'd come in, catch sight of me, and slip out with tears in their eyes, unable to face my suffering head-on.

And then there was a Pakistani lady—a complete stranger. She had only heard about my condition through other staff in the hospital, yet she came every day, driven by a kindness I couldn't comprehend. I had never known her, but her presence was like a warm light cutting through the shadows. She would stand by my side, playing Surah Rahman, her prayers wrapping around me like a comforting embrace, whispering hope into the chaos surrounding me.

"Ya Allah! Cure my brother" she prayed.

Day 23

It was Friday, and my brother arrived wearing a pathani-style kurta. Today, I felt a flicker of clarity breaking through the fog of my illness. As I surveyed my surroundings, I realized with a mix of wonder and despair: I still had all my teeth, yet I was utterly helpless and paralyzed.

Memories flooded my mind like scenes from a movie, vivid and bittersweet. I recalled my childhood, growing up with seven siblings was chaotic and torturous, yet they were the source of my greatest comfort and love. I looked back at the morals and values my Dad and Mom instilled in me with a balance of discipline and affection. Whether it was a stern scolding or a gentle hug, a slap or a warm embrace, each moment was a reflection of their love and dedication to shaping me into a better person.

I reminisced about the visits to Nani's house, the joy of climbing trees with my cousins, and the mouthwatering meals my Mami would prepare—each dish a tapestry of flavors woven with love.

School days followed—a blur of naivety and shyness—where I drifted through, often unnoticed and uncertain. While I managed to achieve good grades, I struggled with the art of making friends and remained an introvert.

College was a similar story; the loneliness seeped in. I drifted through those years without friends, lost in a haze, merely eating, breathing, and sleeping as time slipped away.

But then came engineering, a turning point that transformed my life. I emerged bold and determined, forging friendships that would last a lifetime. The late-night study sessions were more than just hours of academic preparation—they became some of the most cherished memories of my life. The nights were filled with laughter, fueled by endless jokes, punctuated by frequent snacks and the cups of tea at 3 AM outside. These moments of shared camaraderie broke down my walls and transformed me, allowing me to express my thoughts and feelings freely. Gradually, I blossomed into an extrovert, discovering the joy of genuine connections and the freedom of speaking my heart without hesitation.

With my engineering friends, I explored many places across India, from the bustling streets of Bangalore to the serene hills of Ooty and Mysore, from the vibrant heart of Delhi to the misty landscapes of Shimla and Manali. We wandered through Pune, the scenic heights of Mahabaleshwar, and finally relaxed on the beaches of Goa, we toured Malaysia and Singapore, each journey etching unforgettable memories in my heart.

Work shaped me further, forging a thick skin and a resilient spirit. I became a people person, ready to tackle any challenge. My time in Dubai marked another unforgettable chapter. The early struggles were tough, but hard work paid off. After my promotion, life burst open—more friends, more parties, more responsibilities. I thrived in it all, earning awards and becoming a beloved figure. In our annual functions, I'd perform to cheers and applause. I learned invaluable lessons in management and much more from my senior managers and fellow UICs—lessons that will stay with me forever. The hikes, outings, celebrations and adventures forged countless memories, and I felt invincible in those moments; it truly was the best time of my life.

Yet, as evening descended, the atmosphere shifted. I overheard the doctors murmuring anxiously about the dangers of remaining immobile—bed sores and internal infections loomed as threats. They prescribed CT scans of my thorax, abdomen, and pelvis, a necessary step in their assessment.

In the midst of it all, I noticed a familiar figure entering. It was my eldest brother, who had traveled all the way from Saudi Arabia just to be by my side. Our eyes met and held, and for a long, silent moment, the weight of everything we shared—the laughter, the memories—passed between us. Tears welled up in his eyes, and voice trembled as he spoke, "I've never seen you like this before." His words hung in the air, heavy with disbelief and sadness, as he took in the tubes, the machines, the stillness of my once-active body.

He moved closer, resting a hand on my stomach as if to transfer some of his strength to me. In that moment, he became the older brother I had looked up to—the one who had quietly taken on responsibilities, who had been my support in countless ways I had never fully realized.

"Do you remember how our dad endured his own battles with illness? He faced every struggle with strength." He said in a softened voice.

I could see the pain and worry etched in his face, but also a fierce determination to remind me of the legacy we came from. My father had battled his own health issues with quiet resilience, facing each day as it came, never letting despair overshadow his courage. My brother wanted me to remember that strength, to carry it with me in this fight, as if he were passing down a sacred reminder of who we were, of the strength we had inherited.

CHAPTER 13

Lab rat

Day 24

Around 6 AM, a blur of sleep still clinging to me, I caught sight of a senior doctor entering the room with a small group of five or six young men and women. They were medical interns who had come to study me, the subject of their case study. As he introduced me, I felt a strange mix of vulnerability and detachment; I was reduced to a specimen.

The doctor began, his voice steady. "The subject's peripheral nerves are completely destroyed, and he has no mobility." His words felt like a hammer striking my chest. It was now up to them to evaluate and examine me, to piece together the puzzle of my condition.

The first intern, a girl with focused determination, approached. She lifted my leg, tapping my skin with precision. With a small hammer, she struck my knees, testing for reflexes, then used her pen to draw lines on my skin and feet searching for any sign of contraction. Just as she prepared to share her findings, the door swung open, and two more students joined the group.

The doctor repeated the introduction, his voice carrying an air of authority. "What's your diagnosis?" he asked the girl.

"It's GBS," she replied confidently. Guillain-Barré Syndrome. The doctor nodded, confirming her assessment before peppering the group with medical terminology that spun around me, incomprehensible and distant.

One by one, the students examined, mirroring each other's actions. I could hear the doctor's questions, some challenging and others basic, but the medical jargon only echoed in my mind. When a young man faltered on one question, the doctor chided him gently, urging him to study more for the next time.

After what felt like an eternity of probing and discussion, I felt my eyelids growing heavy. I dozed off, the sounds of their chatter fading into the background, a lullaby of voices that drifted away until I could no longer discern when they left.

By now, I had come to realize that expecting empathy or compassion from the nurses was futile. I stopped pestering them with my shaking body or desperate sounds. Instead, I surrendered completely, lying still, an unwilling participant in this new reality. In my silence, I felt a profound sense of resignation wash over me, accepting the weight of my circumstances as I drifted deeper into the haze of sleep.

Day 25 and 26

The reports from the scans arrived, and the news hit like a wave: infection in lungs. A bronchoscopy was necessary. But honestly, what did it matter? Nothing felt significant anymore.

The days passed in a monotonous rhythm, a blend of reminiscing about my past and mourning my present. I drifted between memories and dreams. My thoughts were a mix of nostalgia and grief, each recollection a bittersweet reminder of the life I once lived, now overshadowed by this relentless struggle.

I lay there, feeling the weight of the world pressing down on me, caught in the tension between what was and what could have been. Each tear that fell felt like a silent echo of my former self, a reminder of the dreams and experiences that now seemed so far away.

In the afternoon, a Consulting Specialist, entered with an impossibly bright smile. He stood there, studying me, and asked me to raise my eyebrows and smile. I tried, but my face remained still, a silent testament to my paralysis. Yet, his smile never faltered,

"Don't worry, you will be 100% recovered, just like you were before April 27th." he reassured, adding,

"But it will take time—maybe two years or more—but you will recover completely."

Two years. The words pierced my heart like a sharp arrow, sending shockwaves through my already fragile spirit. Two years like this? Who would take care of me? How will we manage the money? The questions spiraled in my mind, and I felt the weight of despair pressing down harder.

That night, my prayers for death grew more fervent. I lay awake, pleading for release from this suffering, begging for peace, wishing for an end to the torment that had become my existence. I couldn't take it anymore.

In the Dream- *I found myself tied tightly to a bed, panic pour sing through my veins. Two nurses—a male and a*

female—stood beside me, discussing the procedure that loomed ahead. Their voices were clinical, detached, as if I were nothing more than a subject in a lab.

When they finally left, I stared at the restraints, my heart racing as I desperately tried to untie myself. Each pull only tightened the bindings, leaving me trapped. The sounds of steel clashing filled the air, bright lights glaring down on me like harsh interrogators, the clanging echoing like metal sheets being welded. My fear grew with every heartbeat, the reality of my situation sinking in.

Suddenly, I found myself running down the dim corridors of a vast building, adrenaline driving me to escape. I could hear footsteps behind me, the urgency of pursuers echoing in my ears. I spotted a pile of cloth and dove in, hiding my trembling body beneath the fabric. But the sense of safety was short-lived. Strange men approached, their weight pressing down on me as they sat on the pile, making it hard to breathe. I felt strangled, paralyzed by fear, desperate to remain unnoticed.

Just then, a man who looked eerily familiar—like the male nurse—appeared. He reached into my hiding place and yanked me out, dragging me along with the cloths to a nearby room. With a swift motion, he dumped me onto a bed. My heart sank as he left, and I realized I was now lying on top of the man who had sat on me, my body tied to his.

Panic surged within me as I struggled to break free. Each movement was futile, the bindings constricting tighter with every attempt. Fear coursed through my veins as I realized the nurses were preparing to operate on me. I trembled uncontrollably, trapped in a nightmare where escape felt impossible, my body held captive by a web of terror.

Day 27

From the moment I woke up, the nurses were a flurry of activity, bustling around me with purpose. They moved quickly, preparing for the procedure, performing blood tests and X-rays with practiced efficiency. Soon, the specialist arrived, reviewing my records before approaching me with a serious expression. He explained the procedure: they would insert a tube thru the tracheostomy into my lungs to address the infection - which later revealed as thick secretion coming from left lobe.

Once everything was set, the nurse administered the anesthesia. As the darkness enveloped, I felt myself slowly slipping away, surrendering to its grasp. I don't recall dreaming, but when I finally woke, it was late in the evening. My brother had come to visit but I was asleep both times.

In the haze of sedation, I stared up at the ceiling, where I imagined prints of animals, cartoons, and trees dancing. I let my imagination take flight, weaving stories as if I were watching a movie play out on the canvas above. Each figure became a character in my mind, filling the void with fleeting joy.

The Stabilizing

CHAPTER 14

Alhumdulillah

Day 28 to 31

I was up all night, staring at the ceiling, lost in my thoughts until a nurse walked in at 3 AM. Despite the exhaustion, a slow and warm breeze of freshness enveloped me. I turned my head slowly, taking in the room with fresh eyes. It felt as though I'd been floating in some endless, weightless space for so long and now my feet is touching the ground.

My brother's face reflected a sense of stability in my health, and he recited *"Alhumdulillah"* over and over. He connected me to my family via video call, and their faces shone with relief, as if a catastrophic cyclone had finally passed. Indeed, it was a cyclone that had ravaged my soul and washed away my optimism, but now I was recovering. Each day, I began to see more clearly the room around me—a world I felt trapped in, like a bird in a cage.

At 1 PM, the physiotherapist arrived, determined to help me regain strength in my nerves. I focused all my willpower on moving my hands from the wrist, feeling the flow of blood surge through them. Each tiny movement laid a brick of courage in my mind. My legs, however, remained lifeless, but I felt a dull pain and unsettling sensations; any touch from the nurse or slight movement sent tremors through my body. The doctors were concerned about foot drop and began placing splints on my legs, which only heightened my unease.

I would nod and plead with the nurses not to put them on, but they knew better and secured them nonetheless. The pain in my legs created a paralyzing fear, making me tremble whenever the nurses lifted the bed to feed me. I would turn my head in anguish, and they would quickly lower me back down after each meal.

In the solitude of my room, I recalled my brother's words—that I didn't need to perform ablution in my condition and could still pray. This thought sparked my imagination. I envisioned a place surrounded by towering mountains and lush trees heavy with giant fruits. A stream of fresh, cold water flowed through the scene, and I could almost taste its sweetness. I pictured myself standing in that stream, washing my face and hands, and then walking onto the green grass, droplets cascading from my body. The moon shone brightly overhead as I prayed on that grass. Was it just my imagination or a vivid dream? I couldn't tell, but in that moment, I felt at peace, closer to Allah, the Almighty. His full attention was on me, with hundreds of people praying for my recovery—every person I knew and many more who had just heard my story.

Growing up, my mom often told me that Allah is nearer to us than our jugular vein, pointing to the veins located in the neck & I became a living witness to how profoundly and magnificently true this is.

One night, after the nurses finished the cleaning, I found myself lying in discomfort. The nurse, hurried in her work, had placed the pillow carelessly beneath my legs, leaving me in a constant, throbbing ache that ran through my limbs. My body trembled as I lay there, the pain relentless. I wanted to scream, to call for help, but my voice was muted, weak. I was trapped within my own silence, and each small movement only seemed to worsen the ache.

Alone in the dim light of the room, I prayed with all the strength I had left. I prayed for someone to come, someone who could adjust the pillow and ease this unyielding pain. But the minutes passed in silence, the empty room around me feeling as vast and indifferent as the pain itself. Exhausted, I continued praying, my thoughts a quiet plea for relief, until at last, sleep began to settle over.

Somewhere between waking and dreaming, I saw a silhouette of a lady entering the room, her figure softened by a gentle, almost otherworldly light that seemed to follow her. My eyes fluttered open in disbelief as I watched her move with a quiet grace, her steps soft, almost gliding across the floor like a wave. Her presence filled the room with a sense of calm, and although she said nothing, I felt as though she knew exactly what I needed.

Without a word, she came to my side, adjusting the pillow under my legs. A warmth radiated from her touch, soothing the ache that had been tearing at me. As the pillow settled into place, the pain began to ease, leaving in its wake a profound sense of relief. I closed my eyes, surrendering to the peace that washed over me, feeling embraced by something profound and deeply comforting, as though heaven itself had sent a touch of grace to my bedside.

In the following days, the doctors noted my stable condition and decided to begin weaning me from the mechanical ventilator to a controlled mode, eventually transitioning to CPAP/PS.

CPAP/PS stands for Continuous Positive Airway Pressure with Pressure Support. It's a type of breathing support used for patients who have difficulty breathing on their own, often due to weakened respiratory muscles or medical conditions affecting the lungs.

Day 32

Just when I thought I was on the mend, able to raise my palm and wiggle my fingers, a day arrived that shattered that hope, leaving me utterly tormented and devastated.

It began around 4 AM, during the switch in ventilator modes. I felt a wave of warmth wash over me, quickly turning into a suffocating heat. I was drenched in sweat, despite the air conditioning. The room felt like a stifling box, and I couldn't breathe.

Restlessness consumed me as I struggled against the feeling of being strangled by my own body. Hours passed in agony, each moment dragging painfully. When the doctors arrived for their morning rounds, I desperately tried to communicate my distress. I rolled my eyes and attempted to convey the suffocation, pleading silently for them to remove the heavy blanket that only added to my torment. But they were fixated on the monitors, declaring that all readings were normal.

One of the nurses, who had been particularly harsh with me in the past, dismissed my suffering with a condescending tone, claiming, "He is just acting."

Frustration surged within me, and I trembled, feeling utterly helpless. Oh, the pain and suffocation were relentless, and no one seemed to understand.

This ordeal continued until 11 AM when my brother finally arrived. The same nurse, wearing her usual expression of annoyance, pointed at the screens, trying to justify her belief that I was merely putting on a show. But my brother was different; he looked deep into my eyes, sensing the unease radiating from me.

"What's wrong?" he asked gently, encouraging me to point to the source of my discomfort.

He began to guess, first pointing at my legs. I shook my head in frustration. Next, he inquired if it was my body. Again, I nodded no. It became clear to him that something else was troubling me. By then, a few senior nurses and the nursing team lead had gathered around my bed, their expressions shifting from skepticism to concern.

"Is there a problem with the room?" my brother asked. Desperate for relief, I nodded vigorously.

"Is it cold?" he asked. I shook my head, signaling no.

"Is it hot?" I nodded yes, more urgently this time.

As the blanket was removed, I could feel the cool air hit my damp skin. I was drenched in sweat, and the nursing team lead quickly recognized what was happening.

"This usually occurs during a switch in ventilator modes," he explained and immediately called for a standing fan.

When the fan was finally turned on, the rush of air felt like a lifeline. It was as if someone had given water to a parched soul. The cool breeze washed over me, and I felt relief flood through my body. With the air blowing at full speed across my face and body, exhaustion overtook me, and I slipped into a deep sleep.

I don't remember waking up for physiotherapy or even my brother's second visit. The warmth of that fan enveloped me, lulling me into a much-needed reprieve from the turmoil of the past hours. In that moment, the world faded away, replaced by a serene stillness that allowed my weary mind and body to rest.

CHAPTER 15

Farewell, Dear Brother

Day 33

My recovery had reached a plateau. I could now lift my palm and move my fingers slowly, though they lacked strength. It should have felt overwhelming, but instead, despair began to seep in, casting me into a well of resignation—a mindset of "let whatever happen now."

My brother was visiting on a one-month visa, which would expire the next day. The thought of renewing it was overshadowed by the responsibilities waiting for him back home—caring for our parents and other obligations in India. After endless discussions with my brother-in-law, my parents, and family members, including my brother in Riyadh, it was decided that he would return to India to tend to his duties, with a promise to secure another visa and come back to support me within a week.

The prospect of my only source of happiness and comfort leaving me felt shattering. Yet, I found myself enveloped in a thick blanket of detachment, becoming increasingly unmindful of my surroundings. My brother had been staying in my room in Al Nahda but now, considering the reality of our situation we knew we would have to leave Dubai in a few months as my insurance was expiring, and the hospital would not keep me beyond that. Considering that my brother cleared the room putting away everything in boxes.

In my state of despair, I subtly indicated to my brother that I wanted him to throw away all my clothes and shoes. But he was determined to keep even the smallest items, showing me photos of my belongings and asking if we should discard things like my old brush or unused bags and boxes. Each image felt like a weight, deepening my sense of detachment from everything that once mattered.

As evening descended, that feeling of separation from the world intensified. Even as friends and colleagues filled my space with encouragement and hope. I nodded along, pretending to be strong, but deep down, my heart only echoed a silent prayer for release—a longing for an end to this suffering that felt like a heavy shroud I couldn't shake off.

Day 34

My health remained steady, but each time the nurses moved my body left and right for cleaning, pain shot through my legs. I endured it in silence, unwilling to complain. Today was bittersweet; my brother was visiting for the last time before his flight back to India. His face revealed the toll of sleepless night and quiet tears.

I tried to give him strength through my eyes, silently reassuring him. He reiterated the plan for his return, emphasizing that he would be back soon. My brother-in-law arrived, promising to visit every day in my brother's absence, urging me not to worry about anything. Despite their reassurances, the heaviness in my heart was palpable as I bid farewell to my brother.

The day wore on, marked by the routine of physiotherapy, medication, and the pervasive loneliness that filled the gaps between my thoughts. As I lay there, memories of the past swirled in my mind, intertwined with fervent prayers.

Day 35

Now, as if pulled by some irresistible force, my thoughts began to swirl around food—constantly, obsessively. Each memory was a vivid snapshot, a tasting of life itself. In my mind's eye, I envisioned a grand feast laid out before me, a table brimming with dishes that had been my lifelong companions, each bite linked to a treasured moment or loved one. I could almost taste the savory warmth of my mother's and sisters' cooking, smell the comforting spices in Mami and Phuphu's recipes.

My senses came alive as I imagined each dish in exquisite detail: the fragrant, spiced Hyderabadi Biryani, the tender fried mutton, the smoky, juicy grilled chicken. Plates of pizza, lasagna, pasta, and quesadillas danced through my mind, familiar and foreign dishes alike forming an intoxicating, impossible spread.

The meal in my mind grew grander. For starters, I pictured mutton gravy with soft, warm Rulami roti and a bowl of hearty Haleem. The main course became a banquet of three distinct styles of chicken dishes, Hyderabadi chicken curry, Butter chicken and Kolapuri chicken, accompanied by not one but two types of biryani—Kacchi Biryani and Sufiyani Biryani, each with its unique spice and character. And for dessert, a sweet selection awaited: creamy Kheer, a colorful fruit salad, syrupy Khubani ka Meetha, and the rich, buttery Double ka Meetha.

I was lost in the richness of each imagined bite, tasting each meal in my memory as if they could somehow nourish me through thought alone.

Days 36 to 37

I weathered the transition in ventilator modes remarkably well, and now the doctors were ready to take the next step. I was placed on a trial of the T-piece with oxygen, completely removing the ventilator. With every ounce of will I could muster, I breathed in for the first time through the piece, and it felt like a rebirth. A rush of life surged within me, reflected in the renewed movements of my hands.

My brother-in-law jumped for joy, ecstatic to see me off the ventilator. He called our family to share the good news. When my colleagues and friends visited, I couldn't help but show off my newfound strength, lifting my hands and weakly closing and opening my fists. It was a small victory, but it felt monumental.

Suddenly, the nurses' attitudes shifted. They became polite, acknowledging my existence and efforts. With the T-piece, mucus began to accumulate in the throat opening, but to my surprise, the nurses cleaned it often without my needing to ask.

The nurse who once only stared at me had now become attuned to my unspoken discomfort. Seeing my struggle, she brought a piece of paper and a pen, carefully writing out the letters A to Z. She began asking me to nod at the correct letters.

"A, B, C, D, E, F," she recited gently. I nodded at "F."

"Okay, F. Let's continue—G, H, I..." We went on like this, letter by letter, until we spelled out "F A N."

"Oh, you want me to turn on the fan?" she said, her voice light with relief as she moved to fulfill my request.

I should have felt happy, right? Proud, even, for managing to communicate a basic need. But instead, a wave of regret swept over me, drowning any trace of joy. What was the point? I should have spelled,

"KILL ME."

How could I continue like this? Yes, I could breathe, but was this even living? The thought of enduring two years—or more—with a paralyzed body, without a job, without independence, felt unbearable. At an age when I should have been taking care of my parents, they would now have to care for me. The roles reversed, the burden shifted. The shame and despair felt crushing.

Yes, I should have spelled "KILL ME." Because in that moment, it felt like the kinder option than the life seemed ahead.

Days 38 to 39

The days began to pass more quickly, filled with the same routine, inching toward progress.

Yet, my lifeless legs posed a growing concern for the doctors. They introduced an Air Pressure Massager, a device that only intensified my discomfort, tormenting me further.

Somewhere in between, I was taken for an ultrasound KUB (Kidney, Ureter, and Bladder) test—an imaging technique to examine the urinary system. For the first time in what felt like ages, I was brought outside the isolation room. No machines were connected to me; I was breathing in room air. As we made our way to the scanning room, I tried to absorb as much as I could of my surroundings, eager to reconnect with the world I had been isolated from for the past one and a half month. The bright lights and the modern decor of the scanning room stood in stark contrast to my dreary ICU space. I complied diligently with the nurses and technicians' directions, focusing on their voices as a reminder that I was still part of the living world. The scan itself was brief, and before I knew it, I was wheeled back to the ICU isolation room.

As my condition stabilized and my recovery began, the hospital made a grave decision. They recognized that complete recovery of my paralyzed body and muscle strengthening would take months, possibly years, and decided to airlift me to India.

My brother-in-law was furious upon hearing their extreme decision, pacing the room with clenched fists, anger etched on his face. But what could we do? Financially, we weren't prepared to spend thousands of Dirhams or Rupees on an airlift. The hospital assured us they would handle the costs with assistance from HR and management.

After a long phone call and discussion with my brother, he returned to my room and held the phone near my face. I saw my brother, calm and steady:

"Remember, everything happens for a reason, right? Maybe this is for the best." He reassured me that the hospital management would decide on a date and let us know in a week time.

In my mind, I cried at the thought of my lifeless body being taken back to my parents, imagining the devastation it would cause them. A new prayer formed within me: either a miracle would allow me to sit in a wheelchair, or I would die, my body returned to India in a bag. I prayed for both possibilities, haunted by the weight of my situation.

On the morning of June 4th, Sunday, the nurse came in with a question that shattered me further: "How do you feel about going to see your parents and family tomorrow?"

A wave of shock and disbelief washed over me, leaving me utterly numb. My mind struggled to process the reality, unable even to imagine what this experience would entail.

That evening, three of my closest friends came to visit—friends I had grown inseparably close to over the past few months. As soon as I saw them, tears welled up uncontrollably, and memories of our laughter-filled parties and gatherings flashed vividly before my eyes, like a reel of an Instagram story.

"No, no, you're not doing this. Stop it right now, or we'll leave!" one of them said firmly, his voice steady but laced with concern. His words were a mixture of love and tough encouragement, an effort to pull me out of the emotional abyss.

I glanced at my own lifeless body, then at my friend from Al Ain, silently urging him to face the harsh reality with me. His face tightened as he fought to suppress his emotions. Finally, he spoke softly, his voice trembling yet reassuring,

"It's going to be alright."

When my brother-in-law arrived, he was devastated by the news of the airlift scheduled next day. The weight of the situation hung heavy in the air, and despite his anger, we were both left grappling with the reality of what lay ahead.

CHAPTER 16

Airlift

Day 40

This day is etched deeply in my mind and soul, a moment I will carry with me forever. It began in the usual 3 AM cleaning routine, a ritual that had become all too familiar. The assigned nurse asked if she could trim my overgrown beard. I nodded yes, feeling a mix of anticipation and anxiety. As the cold blade glided across my skin, I was flooded with sensations—sharp yet soothing. Surprisingly, the emotional weight that often accompanied during the cleaning was absent. It felt hollow.

A few hours later, two men entered the room along with the nursing team lead—a doctor and a support staff member—here to oversee my airlift from the hospital to Dubai Airport, then onward to India. Their demeanor was reassuring; they exuded confidence and competence.

As the process began, the nurses removed the ECG and glucose connections, followed by the thick tube that had been piercing my left hand vein. Only the feeding tube, cannula in my right hand, and the urine bag remained. For over an hour, I was left to absorb the reality of my impending departure—something I dreaded. But a numbness had settled in; I was emotionally detached from it all.

My brother-in-law, Office HR, a few friends, and my boss, came to bid farewell. Tears welled in my eyes as I attempted to convey my gratitude by lifting my hand. I hoped they understood, but all I could see were their faces filled with concern and hope for my recovery.

The room became crowded with nurses, Doctors, and the two gentlemen. Then came the staff from the Dubai Ambulance, a man and a woman, quick and sharp, likely of Filipino nationality. They transferred me onto the ambulance stretcher, handing my belongings—discharge summary, passport, and glasses—to the support staff.

My heart sank as the wheels of my stretcher began to turn, guiding me out of the isolation room through the large ICU, past nurses and doctors. We passed the waiting area, lined with benches where family members sat. Then came the lobby, where I caught glimpses of everyday life outside these sterile walls. As we approached the elevator, a small crowd of people was already waiting inside. The ambulance attendant, however, spoke with a command that left no room for question. "It's urgent—please clear the lift." One by one, they stepped out, glancing at me with a mix of sympathy and curiosity as they left. The doors closed, and I felt the floor sink as the elevator descended, taking us lower and lower, down to the basement, where the ambulance was ready outside the building with its opened door.

Stepping outside into the sunlight after 40 days was surreal. I felt the sun's heat on my skin, an experience I had almost forgotten. Hospital manager, who had been there with zamzam water on my admission day, ran over to say goodbye, tears in her eyes. But I was already in the ambulance, the doors closing behind her.

Inside of the ambulance was like a miniature hospital, equipped with oxygen, suction devices, and other emergency equipment. On ceiling were rods to hold and support hanging glucose bottles. Several small shelves and boxes to keep the gloves, bandages, syringes and medications. The support staff settled next to me, and the doctor took his place beside the driver. As we drove, I lay still, merely breathing, gazing at the bright hot sky through tinted glass.

We arrived at the airport terminal through a special entrance for emergency vehicles. The doctor and support staff went inside the immigration building to get my passport stamped, while the ambulance staff secured a temporary permit for us to enter the runway. The immigration checks were thorough, and the final check involved a police officer examining me closely. The doctor fielded their questions, and after what felt like an eternity, my passport received the exit stamp, alongside our boarding passes.

The ambulance took us to a medical camp within the airport—a waiting area before the flight. However, the driver mistakenly brought us to the wrong camp at first.

"It was 3B not 3D" cried the other staff.

When we finally entered the correct medical camp, it was empty. Some staff rushed in upon our arrival, and I was carefully transferred from the ambulance stretcher to a bed.

While waiting, the support staff cleared my mucus using a handy suction machine and adjusted the air conditioning to help with my discomfort. Food and medicine were administered, and just as we were settling, the phone rang—our flight was ready, the paramedics quickly transferred me from the camp bed onto a stretcher and rushed to the runway.

Navigating through numerous doors and hallways, we reached a cabin that would drive us to the aircraft. The sudden loud sound of the airplane engine startled me. As the cabin lifted towards the airplane's back door, a steward who knew the doctor, greeted us and asked for our passports and boarding passes. I was lifted onto a small stretcher by a group of men and placed above the passenger seats, in an area that resembled a luggage compartment.

Strapped in tight for the flight, the doctor instructed me to inform him of any air pressure discomfort, assuring me they had a small ventilator on hand. The minutes stretched into what felt like eternity, and when the flight finally took off, I felt nothing—an overwhelming numbness engulfed me. I don't remember evening reciting any prayer.

The flight lasted three and a half hours, and both the doctor and support staff tended to me attentively, using suction devices and adjusting the AC as needed. I should have felt joy at the care I was receiving, but I remained emotionally distant, simply observing the passengers around me as they moved, ate, and used the restroom. It was a large airplane filled with families, featuring seven seats arranged in a 2-3-2 configuration per row.

As the plane landed, I felt the jolt reverberate through my body—the wheels hitting the ground of Hyderabad International Airport. We waited until all the passengers had disembarked, the doctor gave his final instructions to the airport ground staff before leaving to complete the handover formalities. I was lifted onto a foldable stretcher and taken to the ambulance. The transition was rough, and the staff handling me seemed indifferent, heightening my discomfort.

From one ambulance to another and in the midst of the chaos, I heard a familiar voice calling out to me,

"I'm here, and you are with us now, welcome."

It was my brother, his voice laced with a mixture of joy and comfort. A wave of relief washed over me, and tears filled my eyes as I saw him and my eldest sister waiting for me.

In the Hospital ambulance, we sped through the streets of my hometown with the siren blaring, my family following closely behind in another car. Midway, the driver received a call— they'd forgotten to return the portable suction machine. The ambulance made a U-turn, and I began to feel increasingly uncomfortable in the cramped space, which had no proper ventilation.

Just before midnight, the ambulance finally arrived at the hospital after a long drive. My family was waiting for me, and we reunited with tears, smiles, and a shared sense of hope on our faces.

The Homecoming

CHAPTER 17

Pathetic experience

Day 41

The date had changed to June 6th, Tuesday, when my stretcher was wheeled into the emergency room of the hospital. I could hear my brother discussing my condition and history with the doctors. My eldest sister and brother-in-law came closer to my bed, and I proudly showed them how I could lift my right hand high in the air. Their joy was palpable; they praised the Almighty for my progress before leaving.

Once it was settled that I would be admitted in the IMCU, the staff began performing routine blood tests, ECGs, and monitoring my blood pressure and pulse. I felt stable and was breathing normally, with no fever. In my mind, I questioned the need for hospitalization; I just wanted to go home and wait for my nerves to strengthen. But my thoughts were muted, and I lay still.

I was pushed through corridors and into an elevator, finally arriving at the IMCU, which was guarded by security. We entered a lobby filled with small rooms, and I was taken towards the last area on the left, where several cleaning staff were sitting, chatting. Soon, the duty doctor arrived with the admission card and assigned me to a tiny room that barely fit a bed, a monitor, and a single chair. A large window with tinted glass was on the right, while on the left, a small sliding glass window opened to the nurse's desk.

I hated every inch of that room. The transition from the large room in the Dubai hospital to this cramped space in India filled me with frustration and suffocation. Without any insurance, I was certain the hospital would impose exorbitant and unreasonable charges. I shook my hand vigorously, trying to communicate to my brother that I didn't want to stay here, but the doctors insisted on admitting me to monitor how my body would react to the change in location and environment.

Around 1 or 2 AM, when the nurse asked if she could turn off the light, fear gripped me, and I shook my head. She left the light on, and I lay there, tears streaming down my face. This wasn't what I wanted. Exhausted from the emotional and physical toll, I eventually dozed off as I hadn't slept since I left Dubai.

I woke around 7 AM to the sounds of multiple people squeezing into the small room—interns, students, doctors, and nurses—all there to observe me, a patient with GBS. Once again, I was a subject of study. I lay still, not answering their questions as they clicked pictures of me and my reports, murmuring and whispering.

When visiting hours began, my brother arrived, looking exhausted and sleep-deprived. He explained that the doctors advised staying at least a week. Worry crept in about how we would manage the finances. Sensing my anxiety, he reassured me, "Don't worry about the money; we will manage."

Amidst this chaos, I caught a glimpse of someone looking at me before quickly leaving; later, I learned it was my elder cousin brother who, overwhelmed by my condition, left in tears. Minutes later, my parents entered the room, their faces a mix of smiles and pain at seeing their son in such a state. Despite their age, they showed remarkable strength and courage, standing by me, praying and blessing me.

I lifted my right hand to touch my mom. My dad wanted to bless me by placing his hand on my head but refrained, as the doctor advised against it due to infection risks. We all fought to hold back our tears, each of us concealing a volcano of emotions ready to erupt. I wanted to break down, to cry out loud, but somehow, I swallowed it all, locking the storm deep inside.

After visiting hours ended, I was left alone in the room until evening. I lay there, staring out the window, feeling the bright, hot light on my hand while construction noise filtered in from outside.

When the second visiting time began, my sisters came one by one, their faces bright with happiness, offering words of encouragement and hope, assuring me that everything would be alright and that I would recover soon.

"Now that you're with us, you'll see how quickly you'll be fit and fine," they said, their voices trembling as they hid their tears, relieved beyond words to see me alive.

Day 42

I woke to the sound of an old man mopping the room, the day beginning with the distinct chatter and scraping of chairs outside my door. Soon, a nurse entered and started drawing what felt like liters of blood from my body. Now that my hands had life again, I could feel the pain of the needle prick. It was rough and her inexperience showed. She inserted the needle, only to realize she'd missed the correct vein. She tried again—several times—repeating the process with each failed attempt, but I remained still. She used a rubber glove as a makeshift belt on my arm. I couldn't help but think, such a big hospital, and they couldn't afford a proper tourniquet. Afterward, an ECG was performed, attaching electrodes from a machine that looked like an antique, they had no proper or advance machinery.

The old man who was a janitor an hour before is now a nurse carrying with fresh sheets and a gown to replace, his rough handling felt jarring compared to my previous experiences. Since I had completed my treatment course in Dubai, I didn't need any further medications. A young woman then entered, introducing herself as a physiotherapist. She lifted my left leg slightly, placed it back down, and left. I later learned that the hospital charged an astonishing   ₹ 2000 for her two-second action.

Next came the doctors, filing in and out, each documenting something before moving on. A group of three duty doctors frequently entered, and I overheard them discussing plans to remove the tracheostomy, a thought that delighted me, as it was the source of my muteness.

When visiting hours began, my brother arrived and suggested it might be better to move to a rehabilitation center, as the hospital fees were exorbitant. He informed me that he'd spoken with several centers and planned to visit them one by one to decide on my transfer. Noticing my discomfort he immediately asked "Are you feeling hot?" recalling that day in the ICU, I gestured yes, prompting him to request for a standing fan, which the nurse immediately installed next to the bed.

After he left, the doctors continued their rounds, moving in and out, walking in a line like ants, engaged in discussions. With the fan cooling my face, I managed to doze off for a few hours. When I woke, I was being transferred to a new room with functional AC. This room was slightly larger but lacked windows, opening directly into the corridor where I could see other patients, doctors, and nurses passing by.

I lay there for a while until the three duty doctors entered the room along with a nurse. In a swift motion, one of the doctors removed the tracheostomy tube and pressed his thumb over the opening in my throat.

"Say something," he urged. I didn't grasp it at first, but he prompted again, "What's your name?"

A weak, low-pitched sound escaped my mouth: "Mohammed Wasif…"

My voice sounded foreign, as my lips felt frozen and my face still. I moved my jaw up and down, but finally, after 42 long days, I was able to speak. I had hoped "Allah" would be my first word, but nonetheless, I started talking. I asked the doctors for their names one by one and expressed how incredibly happy I was to finally be speaking again.

They used dressing tape to cover the opening in my throat, advising me to limit my speech before leaving. I lay there, praising the Almighty for this blessing, until evening when my brother came for visiting hours.

"What happened? Can you talk now? Does it hurt?" he asked, curious to know if I could talk.

But I initially shook my head no, just for fun. He stood there unable to understand. Suddenly, I blurted out,

"Thank you, brother, for everything you've done."

He burst into tears, holding my hand tightly. We both cried for a few moments, overwhelmed by disbelief. I kept thanking him, but he reassured me he would do anything for me and stepped out of the room in joy.

I then spoke with my mom and dad for the first time, my voice sounding unfamiliar but undeniably mine after such a long silence.

"I'm really very sorry" I said crying, "I made you all go thru this".

They cried along but comforting "It is just a test, we will get past it".

Later, I heard that my dad had distributed boxes of sweets to relatives and neighbors in celebration of my newfound ability to talk.

A noticeable shift occurred in my demeanor; I could now call out to a nurse when I needed something, expressing my thoughts freely. This feeling was exhilarating. I was not fed anything but given IV glucose for strength. As night fell, the ambiance in the IMCU grew quiet and dark, with the lights in the rooms and corridor turned off, except for mine, which I requested to remain on.

Day 43

I woke up feeling a wave of relief wash over me—I could finally speak. A weak smile crossed my face, but it was quickly interrupted by a woman entering the room, asking if I wanted some tea. I declined, frustrated that they didn't seem to understand my condition, especially since I had a feeding tube and couldn't swallow anything.

Soon after, a young boy in a uniform arrived, preparing to draw blood. He began to poke painful needles into my arms, and when I questioned the necessity of these blood tests, he simply shrugged, clearly unaware of their purpose. He then brought the same old ECG machine, and I asked him why I needed an ECG if my heart was fine. He finished his work in silence, treating it as a mere obligation.

Moments later, the physiotherapist came in. She lifted my leg briefly before placing it back down, ready to leave again.

"Hello Doctor, what is your name?" I stopped her asking, after she answered I continued to question what really she planned to do,

"Is this all your physiotherapy session? Just lifting my leg?" Her frustration boiled over, and she twisted my leg sharply, causing me to scream in pain. She blamed me for her lack of care and stormed out.

When my brother arrived, I vented my frustration, insisting that I didn't want to spend another minute in this terrible hospital. He reassured me that we would transfer later that evening. I spent the entire day anxiously awaiting that moment, my impatience growing by the minute.

However, around 7 or 8 PM, my brother returned with disappointing news: there were no available beds at any rehabilitation centers, and we might have to stay another day. This news sent me into a spiral of anger and despair. He then explained that the doctors advised us to move to a regular room instead of the IMCU.

Feeling uneasy, I was wheeled out of the IMCU and into the hospital corridors. We took the elevator to a new floor that felt like a lavish hotel, adorned with bright lights and chandeliers. We moved across rooms with huge wooden carved doors and entered our room, which itself was massive, furnished with sofas, curtains, a TV, a small fridge, and an attached bathroom. But I wasn't impressed—I could sense the hospital was only trying to extract more money from us.

I lay there, restless, listening to my oldest nephew chat about his life and recent events with his cousins, but my eyes remained glued to the door, waiting for my brother to rescue me. Nearing 11 PM, he finally arrived with good news: A Rehabilitation Center had accepted my case, and we would move there immediately. I rejoiced but that wasn't the end of the struggle.

The discharge process stretched on for hours, and just as we were finally about to leave, a tense argument broke out. I had been brought into the hospital wrapped in two sheets, which a nurse had removed. Now, lying on a hospital bed with only a thin gown, we realized the bedsheet and blanket I'd been resting on were also hospital property—and they wanted them back.

My brother argued, "How can we take him out with just a gown?" but the hospital staff showed no leniency.

He fought and offered to return the items once we reached the rehab facility, but they refused and demanded additional payment.

Under the disguise of care, the hospital bill, reached a soaring 2.5 lakhs for just three days, padded with charges for unnecessary tests, repeated ECGs, and consultations that hadn't even taken place. To add, they included staggering fees for the IMCU and the few hour stay in the General room, and physiotherapy session—the worst I had ever experienced.

Yet, it seemed, this amount still wasn't enough to satisfy them. Their behavior was unacceptable after having already drained us financially.

I was deeply angered and frustrated by the hospital's exploitation—fees and subjecting us to harassment, mistreatment, and a complete lack of compassion by their callousness. In a desperate state, I begged my brother to just let them take the sheets, urging him to take me away from this place as soon as possible. After a heated argument, he had no choice but to deposit ₹10,000 to keep the dirty items and later return.

Finally, we left the hospital under the cover of darkness, squeezed into a small, cramped ambulance, heading toward the rehabilitation center.

CHAPTER 18
Rehab

Day 44 – 45

After a pathetic, lamentable and sickening experience of the Hospital, we arrived at the rehabilitation center in the early hours of the night. The building was quiet, and I was wheeled into a large, empty room on the second floor, furnished only with a bed and a bench. As soon as I lay down, waves of pain jolted through my body. After being cocooned in the comfort of ICU beds, my back couldn't adjust to the flat surface, which had a hinge poking uncomfortably. Restless, I cried out to my brother, "Something is not right."

Electric pulses of pain coursed through my nerves, so intense that we feared a return to the ICU might be necessary. Thankfully, a duty nurse arrived and calmed me with an injection. We spent the night in that room, but the next day, after requesting a better bed, we were moved to a smaller room on the newly constructed third floor. This space was more inviting, with well-painted walls, a wooden ceiling, a TV, and an attached washroom. A large window, framed with curtains, offered a view of thick tree branches that shielded us from the sun and let in a gentle breeze.

In the afternoon, I met my physiotherapist, who greeted me with a confident smile. She conducted an extensive session of bed exercises for over 20 minutes, informing me that I would soon be taken to the therapy hall.

"We will take you there on a wheelchair" She said. The idea of sitting up after lying in bed for over a month was overwhelming. I was excited and scared at the same time.

Day 46

After two days of tentative bed exercises, I was finally assisted into a wheelchair. Young boys dressed neatly with contagious smile, wrapped me snugly in a bedsheet and lifted me effortlessly. A strange sensation washed over me; it felt like both nothing and everything. The simple act of moving, of sitting upright, sent a ripple of new sensations through my body—both exhilarating and strangely unsettling, as if I were experiencing my own weight and existence for the first time in weeks.

We went down thru the elevator and crossed the street to enter the building opposite. The street in between had bikes passing, cars parked, people staring, I looked at the bright sky and the green trees with a faint smile, feeling the breeze of life. We took the elevator which was just on the right side of the entrance, a reception on the left with a small waiting area, few large sofas and wall mounted TV.

On 4th floor was the physiotherapy hall, an expansive, open space filled with the hum of activity. Rows of exercise machines, balance balls, tilt beds, bicycles and therapy beds filled the room, arranged in a layout that seemed orderly yet intimidating. Sunlight poured in through the glass walls, casting bright patterns across the floor and offering a panoramic view of Banjara Hills stretching out in the distance. The vibrant world outside felt like a stark contrast to the sterile, clinical environment within.

Almost fifteen other patients were immersed in their own treatments—some struggling through exercises with looks of intense concentration, while others were guided gently by therapists, encouraged with steady hands and calming voices. The hall buzzed with a quiet determination, an undercurrent of shared resolve that was both comforting and overwhelming. I watched as people moved and stretched, their faces a mix of hope and weariness, each of them embodying a battle that was uniquely theirs, yet somehow felt deeply familiar.

Day 47

In the early days of my rehabilitation, every physio session felt like a haunting ordeal. Numb and hollow, I endured the process as my body was mechanically moved—from bed to wheelchair, then to the exercise bed, and back again. Being wrapped in a bedsheet and lifted felt dehumanizing, as if I were nothing more than a piece of furniture being shuffled around the house.

One particular piece of equipment, the tilt bed, left an unforgettable impression. This bed could adjust from horizontal to vertical in varying degrees, and my first experience on it was overwhelming. As I was strapped and gradually tilted upright, a wave of uneasiness surged through my entire body. My pulse skyrocketed past 100 beats per minute, alarming my physiotherapist, and the session had to be halted.

The recumbent bike-cycle, too, became a source of anxiety. I vividly remember my legs strapped on the pedal, my body started trembling, calling out in desperation,

"Doctor, Doctor, can someone stop this? I'm feeling so uneasy!" My mother, standing beside me, tried her best to soothe me, her comforting presence anchoring me in that moment of panic.

Even back in the ward bed, the crushing weight of my situation was inescapable. Yet, amidst the despair, my family's unwavering support became my beacon of hope. Their presence, their words, their silent acts of love—all of it strengthened my resolve to fight and recover.

I often thought back to the words of a nurse on my final day in the Dubai hospital. While feeding me, she had said, "You'll see, once you're with your family, you'll recover very fast." Her words echoed in my mind during those grueling days. They proved prophetic.

With each passing day, surrounded by the love of my family and the encouragement of relatives who visited, I felt a steady but undeniable improvement. What once seemed impossible now began to feel within reach.

Day 48 - 50

My physiotherapist approached each session with great care and dedication, encouraging me to sit, stand, and cycle using the machines. With every movement, I felt my dormant muscles slowly awakening, responding to the gentle yet persistent guidance. The recovery felt almost miraculous—a rapid progress I hadn't thought possible. Alongside it, a newfound sense of willpower surged within me, pushing me to do more, to go further, and to reclaim the strength I once thought I had lost forever.

The entire rehabilitation center - including all the physiotherapist, especially MY physiotherapist, played a pivotal role in my physical recovery. Her meticulously crafted plan and its seamless execution were nothing short of exceptional. She struck the perfect balance, pushing me to surpass my limits without overwhelming me, ensuring that every step of my journey was both challenging and manageable. Her gentle yet firm guidance created a sense of comfort that made the treatment process feel less daunting.

The vibrant atmosphere of the center, filled with the warm smiles and unwavering dedication of passionate doctors, created a sense of hope and positivity. It was a place where even the weight of pain seemed to lift, if only momentarily, replaced by encouragement and support.

After two days, the doctor approved liquids. Slowly, drop by drop, I sipped water for the first time in 48 days, tears of joy streaming down my face. My third sister overjoyed, brought in soup and mango paste which I devoured wholeheartedly.

As my muscles began to regain strength, an intense pain followed, shooting through my nervous system like a bolt of lightning searing its way from head to toe. Each wave of pain left me trembling, my body quivering with the shock of it. But no matter how excruciating each jolt was, I was never alone in those moments. My mother, brother, and sisters stayed by my side, their hands steady on mine, their voices soothing, grounding me through each surge. Their presence was a lifeline, a reminder that even in my darkest pain, I was held in love and strength.

In the quiet of one afternoon, my second sister arrived to relieve my brother, stepping softly into the room. She looked delicate, almost fragile, but there was a quiet resilience in her gaze that I hadn't fully seen before. Despite her petite frame, she approached my bedside with a strength that felt as steady as it was surprising.

At one point, I had slipped too low in the bed, and before I could even ask for help, she leaned over and firmly grasped my shoulders. With surprising ease, she pulled me up, gently yet resolutely, adjusting my position so I could rest more comfortably. I looked up at her, feeling a wave of emotion wash over me. Here was my sister, who I'd always seen as gentle, stepping up with a strength that was both physical and emotional.

In that moment, I realized just how much love can empower us. All my sister's strength wasn't just in their hands but in their determination, their quiet resolve to care for me in any way they could. It was a strength I hadn't expected, yet it filled me with a deep sense of gratitude, knowing they would do anything to ease my pain.

Days passed with family visits that filled the room with laughter and tears, alongside my physiotherapy sessions and the excruciating pain in legs. I started eating soft food but still swallowing was painful.

During this battle, my weight plummeted from 75 kg on day one to just 45 kg. I had become painfully lean, my bones starkly visible beneath my skin, as if flesh had simply been draped over a fragile skeleton. Every joint, every rib, stood out sharply, each one a reminder of the toll my body had endured. I felt like a shadow of myself, reduced to this thin layer of skin over bone.

Day 51

A new rhythm had settled into my days, a structured routine that felt both reassuring and exhausting.

7:00 AM — The familiar ritual of cleaning and fresh sheets. Instead of a nurse it was a ward boy, moved briskly and roughly, but to me, each step was a reminder of progress—a slow but steady movement toward recovery.

9:00 AM — A small tray with semi-solid food arrived, marking another step forward in my journey to rebuild strength. Eating felt strange, a new challenge that required patience as I adapted to textures and flavors again. I savored each bite, no matter how simple, treating it as a quiet victory.

9:30 AM — The physiotherapy sessions began. I was wheeled into the therapy hall that now felt familiar. The sessions were grueling, pushing me to my limits and often beyond. Muscles, dormant and weak, screamed back to life, sending bolts of excruciating pain through my body as if every nerve were awakening at once. But I pressed on, driven by the face of my Physiotherapist, her quiet encouragement like a balm against the physical strain.

11:00 AM to 2:00 PM — I found brief respite in rest. My body, both exhausted and relieved, sank into the bed, and I welcomed the quiet lull of sleep, each hour a brief sanctuary.

2:00 PM — Lunch arrived, another routine that brought a sense of normalcy and hope.

3:00 PM — It was time for the second physiotherapy session of the day, each movement coaxing me to stretch my limits. I pushed forward, often trembling with pain but comforted by the thought that every step brought me closer to reclaiming control over my own body.

7:00 PM — Dinner marked the end of the day's efforts, a moment to gather strength for the night ahead. Afterward, I would settle into bed, drifting into sleep and hoping that tomorrow would bring another inch of progress.

Day 52 - 55

What once felt like a lifeless shell, a body I hardly recognized as my own, was slowly transforming, inching back toward life. I could feel my heartbeat steady and strong, its rhythm like an old friend returning. I could speak again, my voice still faint but growing louder each day, each word a testament to the long journey back. Eating felt like an accomplishment, the flavors igniting my senses, and sitting, even standing with support, seemed like a newfound freedom after weeks of confinement.

"I'll throw this ball, and you should catch it, okay?" my physiotherapist said during one of our sessions, her tone gentle yet filled with a quiet determination. I was sitting there, leaning and weak, barely able to keep my balance, but I nodded. When the ball came toward me, I reached out—and caught it. Not once, but every single time she threw it.

The room fell silent for a moment, eyes turning toward me in surprise. It wasn't often they saw such rapid progress, especially from someone in my condition. Others in the room, many of whom had been working on their recovery for months, looked on as I surpassed milestones that had taken them far longer to achieve.

"You all believe in... what's that word... *dristi*... what is it in English... yeah, evil eye?" my physiotherapist asked with a playful smile.

"Tell your mom to do a prayer to ward it off," she added, her words carrying a teasing warmth. I couldn't help but notice the sharp grin of pride and happiness lighting up her face, reflecting her confidence in my accomplishments.

The credit belonged entirely to the Almighty, whose grace carried me through this journey, and to my physiotherapist, who had gone above and beyond in her efforts. Her dedication, patience, and belief in my potential had helped me break barriers I hadn't thought were possible, igniting a spark of hope and determination within me that grew brighter with each session.

Yet, there were still reminders of my vulnerability. I couldn't control all bodily functions; I continued to pass urine involuntarily, leaving me reliant on others for the simple dignity of being cleaned. Every time I needed help, an unshakable wave of embarrassment washed over me. It was humbling, being so exposed and dependent.

But then, on the day 55, a subtle yet extraordinary change unfolded. A sensation, one I had not felt in so long, stirred in my bladder—a small but clear signal that my body was reawakening, taking back its autonomy. I realized, with a rush of relief and gratitude, that this was another victory. It may have seemed like a small, private triumph to an outsider, but for me, it was monumental. It was my body whispering that it was healing, piece by piece, as I regained a bit more control, dignity, and independence. And with that sensation, I felt hope solidify, anchoring me for the battles yet to come.

Day 56

Each day marked a small yet extensive achievement. I had made remarkable strides, and the progress felt almost surreal. Now, I could sit up on my own, and even stand with support—a sight that left the other patients and doctors watching in surprise and admiration. Where I had once been motionless, now I was beginning to reclaim control, each step and movement proof that recovery was within reach.

As my strength grew, I found myself ready for more independence. And I asked for the urine bag to be removed, eager to experience the dignity of using the toilet with help of my brother. The moment was both humbling and exhilarating, another step toward leaving behind the vulnerability that had once defined my days.

Then, on day 58, another significant milestone arrived: the feeding tube was finally removed. After weeks of relying on liquid nutrition, I could now eat solid food—a simple, liberating act that brought immense relief. With the feeding tube gone, I was free from all the external attachments, unburdened from the reminders of my frailty. I felt a powerful surge of gratitude for these small victories, each one pulling me closer to the life that awaited beyond the hospital walls.

CHAPTER 19

Rebirth

Day 60

As the hours slipped toward midnight, I lay in bed, thoughts drifting to past birthdays. I had given a great importance to this day making each one a grand affair, celebrated with family and friends, and marked by joyous gatherings and cakes, yes cakes—a different one for every group or friend, some years, I'd cut more than six cakes in a single day. Received so many thoughtful gifts, gave return gifts to my parents, brothers, and sisters, showering everyone with a piece of the happiness my birthday brought me. Thinking of this birthday, I felt a mix of gratitude and sadness. The celebration wouldn't be the same, but I was alive to witness it, and that, in itself, was a gift.

Lost in these reflections, I dozed off, only to be gently awakened by my brother right at midnight. He led me to an unexpected sight—six of my friends from engineering, standing by with a cake. They had come all the way to the rehab center, their presence lifted my spirits. Emotional and overwhelmed, I sat up in bed, clapping through the tears, my heart full. I captured the moment on my phone, but its memory would stay imprinted in my mind far longer.

Later in the morning, the warmth continued. My mother arrived with soft sweets, sharing them with that familiar, comforting love, while one of my sisters brought a fresh bouquet, praying continuously for health and blessings. My eldest sister walked in with a massive greeting card, beaming yet holding back tears. The last time she'd seen me, I'd been unable to sit up, and seeing me sitting now, she broke down, hugging me tightly, sobbing, "My brother, you can sit now." Her raw joy left everyone in the room moved.

Calls flooded in throughout the day, bringing with them more love and well-wishes. Despite my doubts, this birthday turned into one of the most memorable I'd ever had. It was a celebration not of age, but of life itself and the beautiful resilience that had brought me this far.

Day 64

June 29 was Eid-ul-Adha that year, and with special permission, we left the rehab to go home a day before, for the celebration. Stepping through the door, I could barely believe I was finally there, among family, not as a patient but as someone reclaiming his life, step by step. When my father saw me, his reaction was something I'll never forget. He cried, unable to hold back his bewilderment, "You surprised me." I knew he had been bracing himself to see me wheeled in on a stretcher or in a wheelchair. Instead, I stood before him, frail but standing on my own two feet, an achievement that seemed to defy the weight of his own fears.

Dad, despite his own frailty and illness, never left my side that day. He had grown weak, his own health burdening him, his hand gripping a walking stick as he moved slowly through the house. Yet, every few minutes, he would make his way to my room, his old, tired frame carrying the same love and strength I had known my whole life. He'd sit nearby, just watching me, as if needing to remind himself that I was really there. He'd ask me simple questions, small talk that somehow meant everything.

Sleeping in a bed at home, after over a year away, was a moment so simple yet profound. Mom and Dad checked on me every fifteen minutes, their worn, old hands helping me up, guiding me gently back down. It was a quiet tenderness, but the sight of their aging faces, marked with lines of worry and love, tore me apart inside. In those moments, I prayed deeply—for the first time not just for strength, but for health, so they could see me whole again.

The morning of Eid was bright and fresh, and although I couldn't go for prayers, I dressed in new clothes and joined Dad for breakfast. His presence next to me, as we shared that small meal, felt like a blessing. As the day unfolded, family filled the house, cousins and relatives arriving, each with tears in their eyes. Everyone had once feared this moment would never come, that I wouldn't be here. And yet, here I was, my frame was weak and thin but alive, standing among them, surrounded by smiles and warm embraces.

The house filled with chatter, laughter, and the aroma of delicacies. We shared meals, exchanged stories, and for the first time in so long, I felt the pure, easy joy of just being with my family. As the sun began to set, it was time to return to the rehab, but I took with me a newfound sense of hope and gratitude. That Eid was more than a celebration—it was a moment of rebirth, a glimpse of the life waiting for me beyond my trials.

Day 69

As I lay in bed, staring at the ceiling, tracing imaginary patterns within the wooden design. I took a deep breath of relief, my heart swelling with gratitude. I looked down at my body—no tubes, no wires, no machines tethered to me. The freedom was overwhelming. I could now turn left or right on my own, a simple act that suddenly felt stupendous. I lifted my hands, clenched my fists, and marveled at the strength I felt returning to them.

In that moment, a vivid dream I once had, came rushing back to me.

In the Dream *-I was approached by TV news channels to shoot an advertisement. It started with me lying weak and lifeless in bed, my hand being lifted into the air only to fall limply. But then, the scene shifted. The next time my hand was raised, it didn't drop. Instead, I grabbed a flying apple and took a bite—a powerful symbol of recovery and vitality. The ad was for a competition with a grand prize for those who had made the best recovery.*

It was just a dream, yet it resonated deeply. That day, holding my phone for the first time in months and managing to unlock it with my own hands felt like my version of grabbing that apple. It was an achievement in every sense of the word.

I called a few friends who had no idea about my illness, and as they heard my unfamiliar, weakened voice, their worry grew. One of them rushed to the rehab center within hours, visibly shaken and struggling to process what he was seeing. *"Kya ho gaya bhai?"* he asked, his tone a mix of shock and relief, grateful to find me alive.

With my newfound strength, I began reconnecting with the world. The phone became my companion during spare moments, helping me pass the time. I started watching videos, voice-texting friends, and updating colleagues in Dubai about my recovery. Each interaction brought me a step closer to reclaiming the life I had known, a life that now felt more precious than ever.

Day 72

The day finally came when I was discharged from the rehab as an inpatient, closing another chapter of confinement that had wrapped itself around my soul. I left the sterile walls and clinical routines behind, taking with me a complex attachment to the place that had been both my prison and my path to healing. As we drove home, each mile brought a sense of liberation, though tinged with uncertainty. Yet, all my doubts fell away as soon as we pulled up to our home.

At the gate, the surprise was waiting. Party blasts, flowers, balloons, and cheerful voices filled the air in an outpouring of joy. My sisters, nieces, nephews, and a few close relatives gathered in a small, intimate celebration. A cake waited to be cut, and they had dressed the house in warmth and welcome. Overwhelmed, I sobbed, but these tears were different—they were filled with happiness and gratitude. My brother stayed close by, steadying me as I took each fragile step.

Mom and Dad wrapped me in the comforts I had longed for—milk and nourishing food, quiet reassurances that made me feel safe and whole. Though my hands grew stronger with each passing day, my legs seemed to know their own schedule, still shaky and requiring patience. We continued daily visits to the rehab, just one session as an outpatient, maintaining the rhythm of recovery that had become second nature. My brother, dedicating himself completely, drove me to each session, staying beside me and offering constant support.

Day 94

The day I first walked on my own was nothing short of miraculous, an achievement that filled me and everyone around me with indescribable joy. I remember the weight of my first unassisted steps, each one a delicate balance of courage and strain. My family watched, holding their breaths, their expressions a mix of disbelief and delight. It was a milestone that felt like the culmination of all those days and nights spent fighting for strength. For the first time, I felt truly empowered—a sense of independence slowly returning, even if only for a few steps at a time.

Around me, the room buzzed with excitement. Smiles, applause, and words of encouragement poured from everyone, celebrating a moment that might seem ordinary to some but was profound to us. My mom and dad looked on with misty eyes, as if their prayers were unfolding before them. My siblings, always my pillars of strength, cheered softly, each whisper and smile filling the room with warmth and pride.

Though I could walk, there were still moments that reminded me how much I had yet to recover. I still needed assistance with basics—getting to the toilet, navigating the bath. But with each passing day, those moments of dependence seemed smaller, mere stepping stones on the path forward. Time began to feel like a friend instead of an obstacle. I could feel its gentle push forward, guiding me one milestone at a time, each day becoming a little brighter, a little stronger, a little more me.

CHAPTER 20

Rise

Day 111

15 August 2023 – I woke up to the blare of my alarm, the sharp rays of morning sunlight piercing through the glass window. As I swung my legs over the edge of the bed, I felt a newfound strength settle in my limbs—a strength hard-won through days of relentless effort and willpower. I sat there for a moment, letting the stillness of the morning carry me back through my journey. A small smile crept onto my face as I reflected on how far I had come.

With determination, I stood up. Though my steps were slow, and my dropped foot caused a limp, I walked steadily towards the washroom. Each movement was deliberate but mine. As I entered, I caught a glimpse of myself in the mirror. The reflection staring back at me was both foreign and familiar. I was still lean, my frame fragile, and my pale skin stretched tightly over bones that were starkly visible.

My face bore the marks of the struggle—skin pulled taut, eyes sunken and unnaturally wide, and their gaze carrying the weight of exhaustion. My lips were flat and still, reflecting the deadened nerves that had silenced expressions I once took for granted. The image was haunting, a reminder of how far I had fallen, but also of the immense progress I had made.

I stared for a moment longer, acknowledging both the scars and the strength they represented.

I used the toilet, brushed my teeth, and took a shower while seated on a chair, relishing the independence of doing these basic tasks alone. Then, I changed into fresh clothes, the fabric feeling like a quiet celebration against my skin.

When I stepped out, I saw my mom standing there, just in case I needed help. Her presence warmed my heart. I smiled at her—a smile filled with gratitude—but my eyes betrayed me.

Tears welled up, spilling over in a wave of mixed emotions. They were tears of relief, for reclaiming small victories; tears of comfort, for the love and support surrounding me; and sharp, painful tears, for everything I had endured to reach this moment.

Gathering myself, I climbed two flights of stairs, reaching the terrace, I stood there under the open sky, bathed in sunlight. The warmth of the sun kissed my face, and I closed my eyes, letting the soft wind caress my hands and cheeks.

I thought I would be flooded with memories of this horrid journey, replaying every moment of pain and struggle. But my mind was blank—eerily, beautifully blank. It felt as if the wind had swept away the weight of the past, leaving only the clarity of the present.

Opening my eyes, I looked out at the vastness before me and realized one thing: I needed to be grateful. Grateful for this moment, for this day, for the chance to stand here, alive, breathing, and whole in ways I hadn't been for months.

Today was a gift, and for that, I would always be thankful.

Freed from the need for therapy sessions, I immersed myself in activities that reignited my passion for life. I baked cakes, selling them to friends who eagerly supported my newfound venture, each order reminding me of the joy in small, creative accomplishments. I cultivated a modest garden in the backyard, watching with pride as seeds transformed into green shoots, mirroring my own journey of renewal. I even launched a YouTube channel, creating educational videos aimed at helping others improve their English. Sharing my knowledge felt meaningful, a way to give back and reconnect with the world.

Desperate to return to normal, I pushed myself too hard, twisting my dropped foot and adding to the already excruciating pain. My brother, both angry and concerned, spoke up:

"Why are you rushing? If you fall again, I won't help you—I'm telling you now."

His voice softened, but his frustration was clear. "Anyone else would still be in bed, taking time to recover. But you... you just won't listen."

I understood his worry, even his anger, as he watched me struggle against my own limitations. But I knew, deep down, that I had changed. This experience had given me a strength and willpower I hadn't known I possessed. I thought of the words from the holy Quran: *"Allah does not require of any soul more than what it can afford."* In this journey, I had found that strength within myself, a resilience that Allah knew was there all along.

Despite the hardship, the path to recovery took nine months and I emerged whole, strengthened by the grace of Allah, the unyielding prayers of loved ones, and the unwavering dedication of my brother, who stood by me through every step, setback, and triumph.

Marking a year since I fell, I celebrated in a way that words alone couldn't capture. I traveled with my mother to the sacred city of Makkah to perform Umrah. There, in the presence of the Kaaba, I prostrated in gratitude, asking for forgiveness and offering thanks. It was a profound moment of peace, a full-circle realization of all I had been given—and a renewal of faith in what is yet to come.

Epilogue

Looking back on these months of struggle, pain, and hope, it's hard to believe how far I've come. What began as a sudden collapse spiraled into months of confinement, battles with my own body, and countless moments of doubt. But it has also been a journey of unexpected strength, deep faith, and unbreakable bonds with those around me. Every small victory, from my first steps to the ability to simply eat on my own, felt monumental. Each milestone reminded me that life, in all its fragility, is a gift.

I am filled with gratitude for everyone who has been a part of this journey. My family—my parents, siblings, and loved ones—held me up when I had no strength of my own. My brother's unwavering support, my mother's gentle care, and the constant prayers from everyone around me became the foundation of my recovery.

The medical teams who worked tirelessly—every doctor, nurse, technician, administrator, HR professional, manager, and even the support staff. The friends who brought laughter and encouragement. The colleagues, friends, and team members in Dubai, who kept in touch and provided invaluable moral support. The rehabilitation center, for their unconditional care in strengthening my backbone- literally, and even the strangers who kept me in their thoughts—all these souls contributed to the miracle of my survival.

In the midst of hardship, my faith in Allah grew stronger. When I traveled to Makkah, standing before the Kaaba, I was overcome by the mercy that had carried me through. I prostrated in gratitude and repentance, recognizing that this journey had not only tested my body but had also transformed my spirit. It was there that I promised to live my life in service to others, to use my story as a reminder that even the darkest trials can be met with light and faith.

As I continue to rebuild, each day feels like a second chance. I no longer take the simple joys for granted—the ability to walk, the taste of food, the warmth of a hug. I know there may still be challenges ahead, but I now carry with me a resilience forged in those hospital halls, a gratitude that deepens with every passing day, and a renewed purpose to live meaningfully.

This journey has taught me that while life is unpredictable, we are stronger than we realize, especially when surrounded by love, faith, and determination. And as I close this chapter, I look forward with hope, ready to embrace whatever comes next, knowing that every breath is a blessing, and every step forward is a victory.